WILLIAMSBURG RESEARCH STUDIES

WILLIAMSBURG RESEARCH STUDIES

Travelers in
Tidewater Virginia

1700-1800

A BIBLIOGRAPHY

Travelers in Tidewater Virginia

1700-1800

A BIBLIOGRAPHY

By

JANE CARSON

COLONIAL WILLIAMSBURG
Williamsburg, Virginia

Distributed by
THE UNIVERSITY PRESS OF VIRGINIA
Charlottesville

FOREWORD

WILLIAMSBURG RESEARCH STUDIES is a series of specialized reports prepared in the research program of Colonial Williamsburg. For almost forty years this program has sought to fulfill a dual objective: to supply the day-to-day information essential to the accurate preservation and restoration of Virginia's colonial capital, and to supplement the interpretation of Williamsburg with studies broader in scope but as detailed in content. The series will make available in inexpensive form those studies of widest interest to students of the era and locality.

To inaugurate the series, we have chosen seven reports from the files of the Research Department. These studies originally were for internal use only; some are largely compilations of the documentary sources relating to a subject, and others are more interpretive. Future titles will appear as research projects are concluded and will include contributions from the fields of architecture, archaeology, hand crafts, and the decorative arts.

Edward M. Riley
Director of Research

Here in Williamsburg, where we try to restore
some of the atmosphere of the eighteenth-century town
along with its physical appearance, we turn repeatedly
to contemporary records for help in re-creating "the feel
of the times." I have found travelers' accounts especially useful in social history because they often record
vivid and detailed first-hand impressions. This annotated
bibliography, therefore, is a guide to a specific kind of
historical source material (the travel account), covering
a limited period (the eighteenth century) and a limited
area (Tidewater Virginia). Since it was prepared for the
use of historians in the Research Department of Colonial
Williamsburg, special attention is given to descriptions
of the colonial capital; these descriptions, however, like
the bibliography itself, are limited to eye-witnesses.

The chief occupational hazard of the bibliog-
rapher is the impossibility of achieving absolute precision in definition. His decisions about what to include are usually arbitrary, and mine are admittedly so.
A word about method is accordingly in order.

To me, "travel account" means a written record
of a personal visit--not only the formal traveler's journal or memoirs prepared for publication, but also the informal diary or letter. Robert Beverley's History and
Present State of Virginia, 1705, for example, is excluded
because I classify it as a history of the seventeenth century written by a native Virginian, but Hugh Jones' Present
State of Virginia, 1724, is included because he lived here
only five years and wrote largely from his own observation.
William Byrd's secret diaries are included because he was
away from home a great deal of the time, and they tell us
almost as much about Williamsburg as about Westover; yet
John Blair's diary, valuable as it is, is excluded because
he was at home in Williamsburg when he made entries in it.

Gazetteers, atlases, histories, and promotional
tracts are excluded unless the author was an observant
traveler as well as a compiler. Most of the geographical
books describe Virginia's natural resources, agricultural
products and trade; some of them contain useful summaries
of economic data and statistical reports; a few of them
(especially those published after 1763) examine the question of Virginia's place within the British Empire and,

in masterly essays, present the author's views on imperial
policy. Users of this bibliography who wish to consult
compilations, in addition to the sources from which their
information was borrowed, will find them conveniently listed
in Thomas D. Clark, ed., Travels in the Old South: A Bibliography (University of Oklahoma Press, 1956).

Together with books and pamphlets, I have annotated
articles in periodicals and manuscript materials. The reader
will notice that some of my travelers did not come to Tidewater Virginia; each of these entries represents my hopeful
pursuit of a false lead, suggested by an inexact title, and
I have included them to warn other miners from lodes of fool's
gold.

For printed materials, the edition cited is the
earliest or the best in the collections at Colonial Williamsburg or the College; for other editions, see Clark, Travels.
Repositories of manuscript materials are cited immediately
after the other bibliographical data.

My own bibliographical leads came from a variety
of sources. Section 48 of the Harvard Guide lists the
best accounts--classics in travel literature. William
Mathews, American Diaries: An Annotated Bibliography of
American Diaries prior to ... 1861 (Berkeley, 1945) includes
everything that had been printed in books and periodicals
when the compilation was made and is an especially useful
check on the short, fugitive diary. In 1941 Park Service
historians on the Yorktown staff compiled and mimeographed
"A Bibliography of the Virginia Campaign and Siege of Yorktown, 1781"; this is well annotated and includes journals
and memoirs of participants in the campaign. Just as I was
completing my collection of titles, the University of Okla-
home Press got out their long-awaited bibliography of Travels
in the Old South, which includes nearly all the books and
pamphlets on my list. Moreover, in each entry the compiler
reviews the author's background, point of view and southern
itinerary and painstakingly lists all the various editions
of the book. I thought it advisable to eliminate duplica-
tion of information so well arranged and so readily available; therefore, I have indicated in my entry the corres-
ponding reference in Clark and confined my annotations to
the author's Tidewater Virginia experience.

Two compilations of selections from travel
accounts were used in the preparation of this bibliography. Twenty-six of my entries are included in the
Colonial Williamsburg Research Report, "General Description of Williamsburg," prepared in 1942. A. J. Morrison,
ed., Travels in Virginia in Revolutionary Times (Lynchburg:
J. P. Bell Co., 1922) contains ten of them.

The most useful index to Virginia periodical
literature is, of course, Earl G. Swem, comp., Virginia
Historical Index (Roanoke, 1934-36). The new Index to
the Pennsylvania Magazine of History and Biography, prepared by the Historical Society of Pennsylvania, led me
to several short accounts that I wouldn't have found
without it.

No exhaustive coverage of manuscript sources
has been attempted. I have checked through printed guides
to manuscript collections in this country and searched
manuscript card catalogues in the libraries visited in
our "dragnet" operation. All journals and letters discovered in this way are included. Finally, there are
the items unearthed by serendipity in the course of the
past year's reading and research in social history.

During the century when Williamsburg was "the
Metropolis" of Virginia, more than 300 travelers visited
the colony and recorded their impressions of it. Approx-
imately two-thirds of their travel accounts contain descriptions of the Tidewater area; these are the titles
annotated in the present bibliography.

Fifty-one percent of the visitors came during
the war years, 1765-1783. The first third of the century
brought fourteen percent of the total number, the next
thirty years accounted for twenty percent, and fifteen
percent came after the Revolution. More than half the
number began their trip by crossing the Atlantic, almost
seventy percent of them from British ports--sixty Englishmen, six Scots and three Irishmen. France sent us thirty-
one visitors, twenty-five of whom came with Rochambeau's
army. Also from continental Europe were seven Germans and
one Swiss. Fifty-one of our guests lived in other American
colonies--seventeen in New England, thirty-three in the
Middle Colonies, and one in the lower South. Twenty-two

Virginians traveled about within the colony and described other areas than their homes.

Reasons for coming to Tidewater Virginia
varied considerably. Seventy-five travelers came with
one of the armies converging on Yorktown in 1781.
Thirty-six were missionary-evangelists, predominantly
Quakers but including also Methodists, Moravians and
Anglicans, interested only in doctrinal matters. About
forty were in search of business opportunity--profes-
sional men, artisans and merchants as well as potential
planters. Ten were government agents preparing official
inspection reports or attending to other public business.
Ten were scholars, scientists or geographers collecting
precise information for publication. Four were prisoners
of war. Twenty-two might be classified as tourists.

The educational background and experience of
the more discerning authors, whose broad interests are
reflected in their thorough coverage of the Virginia
scene, cannot always be determined. It can be said,
however, that seven of the better accounts were written
by doctors, five by preachers, two by lawyers, two by
actors, one by an architect, three by tutors, three by
indentured servants or apprentices, two by college
students, five by women, and two by young girls.

As one would expect, the best reporters were
Englishmen, who readily saw in Virginia contrasts and
comparisons with a similar society at home. In the first
part of the century the Rev. Hugh Jones shares honors
with the Swiss Michel. In the middle period the
Rev. Andrew Burnaby stands alone as a first-rate observer.
In the decade of the seventies, as political tensions
increased, there are J. F. D. Smyth, Nicholas Cresswell
and Thomas Anburey--less reliable reporters and less
sympathetic analysts of Virginia society and ideals.
During the Virginia Campaign of 1781 the English military
diarist yields place to the French and German. After the
Peace of Paris, 1783, the best British descriptions of
the American scene, less discerning than earlier ones,
are represented by young Robert Hunter and Isaac Weld.

Frenchmen showed little interest in Virginia until after the Seven Years' War. The anonymous agent of the French government who visited the American colonies in 1765 was an excellent reporter of personal experiences as well as official data. Officers in Rochambeau's army who traveled about in Virginia immediately after the Siege of Yorktown--men like Chastellux and Robin--wrote enthusiastic comments on the way of life in the new republic. Those who came to America while the revolution was in progress in France were looking for beneficial effects of the newly-achieved liberty in society and government, and they interpreted the evidence according to their attitudes toward events at home. Thus the Jacobin Brissot de Warville saw little in Virginia beyond the degrading effects of slavery while a refugee from the Jacobin régime, Moreau de St.-Méry, found Virginia society attractive and congenial.

Other continental Europeans seldom visited America, but when they did they were intelligent and precise observers. Francis Louis Michel came at the beginning of the century to spy out the land for a future Swiss colony and wrote a report for his fellow-countrymen that told prospective settlers all they would need to know about Virginia in order to live here in contented prosperity. After the Revolution, Baron von Closen and Dr. Johann Schoepf stayed on to write travel accounts that meet the reporting standards set by Michel four decades earlier.

Visitors from other colonies who were neither soldiers nor missionaries were usually good, if critical, observers--notably young Josiah Quincy, Philip Fithian and Ebenezer Hazard. The most widely traveled of all Virginians, William Byrd II and George Washington, kept diaries that supply the most useful grist for the mill of the social historian.

The subject matter of these 200-odd travel accounts varies, of course, according to the personal interests of the author. Everyone commented on travel conditions--shipboard accommodations, roads, ferries, inns, private lodging. Tributes to Virginia hospitality are almost universal, though some visitors found it more overwhelming than comfortable. They agreed that food

and drink were of good quality, plentiful, and varied in
planters' homes and in Williamsburg taverns, but most of
them complained about the fare in ordinaries along the
roads.

Nearly everyone was favorably impressed with
the climate, scenery and natural resources of the colony.
Foreign visitors almost invariably described native animals that were new to them, notably the rattlesnake, the
humming bird and the opossum, and often wrote about Indian
life even when they had not seen an Indian in their travels.
Though they did not always approve of the tobacco economy,
they usually described it. Superficial observers chose
large plantations as typical examples, and the Virginia
planter--even when he was also the host--emerges from the
composite picture an idle, domineering, julep-drinking,
hard-riding and hard-gambling country squire, whose charming wife, obedient children and horde of slaves ministered
to his every comfort. Analyses of the institution of
slavery emphasize the living conditions of the slave--his
diet of corn bread, his nakedness, his long hours of ar-
duous labor--and the effects of the system on the master.
The author's emotional reaction to the system is usually
included in his description of it; Frenchmen, for example,
often saw the Virginia Negro as one of Rousseau's noble
savages, while Quaker missionaries saw only the moral deg-
radation of master and slave alike. No one attempted an
analysis of the economic efficiency of the system.

Summary descriptions of the planter's way of
life emphasize its independence, luxury, leisure and
loneliness. Only in the diaries of persons who lived
on a plantation for several months (Fithian and Harrower,
for example) does the reader find a picture of the hard-
working, orderly existence of efficient and responsible
masters and mistresses of Virginia households, great and
small. Virginia hospitality, Virginia speech, Virginia
horses and the "planter's pace," Virginia ham and hot
bread, peach brandy, julep and grog--all appear in
travel literature as established traditions, but nobody
said "Boo" about fried chicken.

While almost everyone commented on some facet
of the Virginia economy and society, only when he was in
the capital did the traveler usually write about the system

of government. Since these sixty Williamsburg visitors
are of special interest to us at Colonial Williamsburg,
I have prepared the following descriptive analysis of their
travel accounts with a supplementary index to them in the
appendix to this report.

In the period between 1700 and 1750 there were
fifteen Williamsburg visitors, most of whom came from
Great Britain. Three were missionary-evangelists who
were received by the governor (Nicholson or Gooch) and
entertained by Commissary Blair; therefore, they have
more to say about the college than any other Williamsburg institution. Only one preached here; the great
Whitefield listened to Blair's "edifying" sermon on
Saturday and, on the Commissary's invitation, conducted
the Sunday morning service "to the Satisfaction and Pro-
fit of many." Other Britishers included two writers, a
professional actor and wit, an official on an inspection
tour, a young soldier in search of a plantation site
where he might beat his sword into a ploughshare, a
physician eager to establish a Virginia practice, and
a scholar who left us our best contemporary description
of Williamsburg. This was Hugh Jones, professor of
mathematics at the College for four years.

Continental Europe sent us only one visitor
early in the century--Francis Louis Michel. When he
was in Williamsburg in 1702, the town was just being
built and he illustrated his descriptions with sketches
of unfinished buildings. He was present for the Williamsburg ceremonies at the death of William III and the
accession of Queen Anne and wrote a detailed and vivid
account of them on the spot.

Virginia travelers of the period include the
planters William Byrd II and "King" Carter, whose official
business brought them to the capital several times a year
for three decades. Carter's diary is concerned almost
entirely with plantation-mercantile affairs at Corotoman,
but there is incidental information about his travel routes,
living arrangements in town, and government business. Byrd,
of course, is our best source on life in Williamsburg during
"Public Times."

From the middle of the century to the beginning
of the Revolution, six Britishers visited Williamsburg. Two

were in search of business opportunity: Dr. J. F. D.
Smyth wanted to practice medicine; Daniel Fisher, inn-
keeper and merchant, did not succeed in either business
because he quarreled with every Virginian he met--with
the single exception of Nathaniel Walthoe. Both were
unusually colorful characters, and their journals furnish
excellent source material. The Rev. Andrew Burnaby was a
critical and penetrating observer of manners and customs,
buildings and institutions everywhere he went, and his
book of travels affords interesting comparisons with
other American towns. Another British "tourist" of this
period, Lord Adam Gordon, has the distinction of being
the only Williamsburg visitor who approached the town
from the South.

        Two foreign travelers in the third quarter of
the century came from continental Europe. The anonymous
agent of the French government who was investigating the
British colonies immediately after the Seven Years' War
attended a ball at the Palace when he was in Williamsburg
and heard Patrick Henry's "Caesar-Brutus" speech. An
Italian wine merchant, Philip Mazzei, came to Virginia
to introduce grape culture and stayed on to become a
friend and neighbor of Jefferson and to take part in the
Revolution.

        Virginia travelers of the period include two
members of the House of Burgesses, George Washington and
Landon Carter. Washington's diaries and account books
contain no descriptions, but they tell us how he traveled,
where he slept and ate when he was in town, what "clubs"
he attended, what amusements he enjoyed, and who entertained him. Carter, like his father, tells us little of
Williamsburg, but his diaries contain one good description
of procedure in the House of Burgesses. Jefferson's
Williamsburg experience belongs to this period, but we have
little direct information about his student life because
his private papers burned in the Shadwell fire of 1770, and
only in later reminiscences did he refer to the Williamsburg
years. (His governorship, of course, belongs to a later
period.) Another Virginian, Col. Hudson Muse, tells us in
a single letter that he came to town solely to enjoy the
theatre--and he did.

The other colonies sent us only one articulate
guest, young Josiah Quincy, who made a sea voyage to
Charleston for his health and returned to Boston in a
leisurely overland journey. Since he was already a famous lawyer-patriot, his critical interest in Virginia's
"aristocratic" system of government absorbed his whole
attention in the colonial capital.

During the Revolution we had nineteen visitors,
only three of whom were not soldiers. An Englishman,
Nicholas Cresswell, came seeking his fortune, but he
arrived in 1777 and found no business opportunity for an
avowed loyalist; his travel account, therefore, is colored
by his disappointments and frustrations. A New Englander,
Elkanah Watson, was merely passing through on an errand to
Charleston. The third, Ebenezer Hazard, was making an
official survey of the postal service; but he was a historian as well as an official, a trained observer of wide
interests, and his description of Williamsburg during the
Revolution is the most complete and discerning I have seen.

Of the sixteen soldiers, one was Henry Hamilton,
"the Hair Buyer," who had been taken prisoner in the West
by George Rogers Clark. His account of life in the Public
Gaol is the source of most of our information about it.
The remaining fifteen are the most articulate of the
soldiers who came to Williamsburg with one of the armies
converging on Yorktown in the late summer of 1781; two
were British, four Americans, nine continental Europeans.
The best reporters were either Frenchmen who came with
Rochambeau or German mercenaries. While they were in
winter quarters in Williamsburg, several of these men
traveled widely in Tidewater Virginia--notably Chastellux,
Doehla and von Closen. (Chastellux, unfortunately, did
not describe Williamsburg in even one lone sentence.)

After the British capitulation at Yorktown,
thirteen travelers in post-war Virginia visited the
former capital. The best observers in this group were
the two who came from continental Europe to study the
new republican societies in America: the French philosopher, La Rochefoucauld-Liancourt, and the German surgeon,
Dr. Schoepf, who came with the Hessian troops in the
British army and stayed on after the war to tour the

country. British nationals continued to visit us after
the war. Two of them were young Londoners collecting
war debts due their fathers' mercantile houses, who
traveled together and spent part of a winter in Virginia--
Hadfield and Hunter. Another young man came from Dublin
on a grand tour to complete his education. This was
Isaac Weld, who was horrified at the informality in the
manners of the students at William and Mary and drew "a
melancholy picture" of the little town of Williamsburg.
Latrobe, architect-engineer, did most of his professional
work in Norfolk and Richmond; he visited Williamsburg,
however, and commented on its architecture, though he
did not sketch any of the buildings here.

American visitors in this period included
Noah Webster, who gave lectures in Williamsburg and
Richmond on his grand southern tour of 1785. Jedidiah
Morse came at about the same time, collecting data for
his geographies. His hypercritical comments on Williamsburg society drew immediate fire from St. George Tucker,
whose open Letter...to the Reverend Jedediah Morse was
the occasion for our best formal description of the town
written by an inhabitant.

Only three Virginia travelers in their home
state have left descriptions of the colonial capital.
One was a student at William and Mary, David Watson. An
itinerant Methodist minister whose circuit included
Williamsburg mentioned a sermon in the Capitol. And a
typical tourist wrote a facetious account of a day in
the ruins of the Old Capital and included among them
Mrs. Campbell, "a little old Woman, about four feet
high; & equally thick, a little turn up Pug nose, a
mouth screw'd up to one side..." and with a manner as
cold as her parlor.

If the traveler came direct to Virginia from
a transatlantic port, his ship entered Hampton Roads and
deposited passengers and goods at a port on one of the
Virginia rivers. Early in the century the traveler
landed at Hampton, Queen's Creek, Yorktown, Urbanna, or
Hobb's Hole. Later Norfolk, Alexandria, and planters'
wharves along the Potomac were becoming more popular
ports of debarkation. Sometimes a pilot boat or river
sloop met the ocean vessel in the Roads and received
passengers and goods for transfer to river ports.

If he came to Williamsburg overland from the North, having landed at Boston or Philadelphia perhaps, he usually crossed the Potomac at Alexandria and followed the road through Dumfries, Fredericksburg, Port Royal and Hobb's Hole or took the more direct route from Fredericksburg through Caroline County.

For river travel, visitors used planters' sloops, canoes, barges, bateaux or yawls. On land travelers usually rode horseback, and ferries transported horses and riders across the Tidewater rivers. (Roads and regular ferry points are marked on the Fry-Jefferson Map of 1755.) Ferryboats varied in size according to the needs and resources of their owners. The typical ferryboat in use at a regular ferry point was a scow, which would accommodate a heavily loaded wagon as well as horses and men. Occasionally a visitor rode with his planter host in a chaise, carriage or horse-drawn chair for short trips within the peninsula where he was staying. I have not discovered an instance of their crossing a river in a ferry-borne carriage; they may have done so, for the larger ferries regularly carried wheeled vehicles in sufficient numbers to require legislative regulation of rates.

Sometimes we find a traveler using a hired vehicle. Burnaby, for example, hired a chaise in Yorktown for his trip to Williamsburg, and the anonymous Frenchman "hired a Chair" in Williamsburg "and took a ride to Jameses City." A few of our visitors traveled on foot, carrying light packs of equipment and food; these were usually missionaries or continental Europeans accustomed to hiking in their own countries. Visitors often commented on the fact that only servants walked in Virginia.

Soldiers coming to Yorktown in 1781 followed a different travel pattern. The earlier arrivals marched overland to the Richmond area--Wayne's troops, for example, joined Lafayette's army at Fredericksburg. In September Rochambeau's and Washington's men arrived via Head of Elk, Maryland, having marched there from New York. The French fleet brought them down the Chesapeake, and and they disembarked at Jamestown.

And so they came, then as now--soldiers, missionaries, scholars, doctors, lawyers, merchants, teachers, actors, students, servants, women, children.

October, 1956   Jane Carson

Travelers in Tidewater Virginia

1700-1800

A BIBLIOGRAPHY

1. Anon.

    A Detail of Some Particular Services Performed in
    America during the Years 1776, 1777, 1778 and 1779.
    Compiled from Journals and Original Papers, Supposed
    to be Chiefly Taken from the Journal kept on Board of
    the Ship Rainbow....New York: Privately printed for
    Ithiel Town, 1835. 117 p. First published in Navy
    Chronicle, XXII (1814), 267-296, 353-400.

    Factual account of the voyage of the Rainbow,
    which convoyed troops from New York to the Chesapeake
    in May 1779, took Gosport, Portsmouth and Norfolk,
    and returned to New York at the end of the month.

2. Anon.

    Diary of French naval operations in America, Jan-
    uary 5, 1779-September 2, 1782. 281 p. Manuscript
    Division, Library of Congress.

    A good general account of the Yorktown campaign,
    written from diary entries by a French officer who
    came to the Chesapeake with de Grasse's fleet and
    served throughout the siege.

3. Anon.

    The Expedition of Major General Braddock to Virginia...
    Being Extracts of Letters from An Officer in One of
    Those Regiments to His Friend in London....London:
    Printed for H. Carpenter, 1755. 30 p.

    The author, one of the seamen ordered by
    Commodore Keppel to the Ohio, saw only the Valley of
    Virginia.

    Clark, Travels, I, #233

4.   Anon.

"Itinerary of the Pennsylvania Line, from Pennsylvania to South Carolina, 1781-1782," <u>Pennsyl-
vania Magazine of History and Biography</u>, XXXVI
(1912), 273-292.

     Brief daily entries in the diary of an uniden-
tified soldier in Wayne's command. The itinerary
included Yorktown.

5.   Anon.

Journal, in French, of the operations and marches
of the French and American forces in the campaigns
of 1780 to 1782. MS HM-578, Huntington Library.
Photocopy in Colonial National Historical Park.

     Detailed account of the operations of the
French fleet in and around the Chesapeake August-
October, 1781.

6.   Anon.

"Journal of a French Traveller in the Colonies,
1765," <u>American Historical Review</u>, XXVI (1921),
726-747; XXVII (1922), 70-89.

     The manuscript is in the Archives of the Serv-
ice Hydrographique de la Marine, vol. 76, no. 2.
Pages 1-54, the English portion of the journal,
extend from December 4, 1764 to September 7, 1765.
The writer has not been identified; he was a French
Catholic, probably an agent of the French government,
but not the Pontleroy who came to America in 1764.
He was a discerning observer, comparable to Burnaby
in his breadth of interest. From April to June he
was in Virginia, with headquarters at Portsmouth,
where he was detained until the arrival of funds
from Philadelphia, and spent the waiting period going "to different parts of the Country by way of
amusement"--to Norfolk, Williamsburg, Hampton,

Yorktown, and Jamestown. In Williamsburg from
April 25 to May 14 he stayed at Mrs. Vobe's, where
William Byrd III and others in town for Public Times
spent their days and nights gambling, "Carousing and
Drinking"; after three days, he was "heartily sick"
of the noise and the crowds. He was again in Wil-
liamsburg May 30, when he heard Patrick Henry's
Caesar-Brutus speech; his account of it and of the
Burgesses' reaction to it is especially interesting
to the historian because it contradicts the tradi-
tional interpretation. The following Tuesday,
June 4, he attended the King's Birthnight ball at
Governor Fauquier's invitation and left Williams-
burg the next day, traveling to Maryland via New
Kent, Hanover and Port Royal. In Hanover he noted
Henry's great popularity with his constituents.

7.   Anon.

Journal of the Siege of York-town as recorded in
the hand of Gaspard de Gallatin and translated by
the French Department of the College of William
and Mary. Printed Washington: Government Printing
Office, 1931 (U.S.Congress, 3d sess. Senate Doc. 322).
48 p.

     Day-by-day description, listing casualties,
captured property and other statistics. Includes
text of surrender terms and Washington's General
Order of October 20, 1781.

8.   Anon.

Letters of Brunswick and Hessian Officers during
the American Revolution....Translated by William
Leete Stone. Albany: J. Munsell's Sons, 1891.
258 p.

     A letter written in Staunton, Virginia, June 1,
1779 describes the activity of soldiers with their
gardens and poultry, the church and theatre erected
by British soldiers, and comments on Virginia tobacco.

Clark, Travels, I, #315

9. Anon.

    The Operations of the French Fleet Under the Count
    De Grasse in 1781-2 as Described in Two Contempora-
    neous Journals. [Ed. by John D. Gilmary Shea.]
    New York: Bradford Club, 1864. 216 p.

        Neither author has been identified, but appar-
    ently both were well informed eye-witnesses to
    French naval action in the Chesapeake. There are a
    few general comments on Virginia people.

    Clark, Travels, I, #284

10. Anon.

    "Siege of York and Gloucester, Virginia," Magazine
    of American History, VII (1881), 222-224.

        A brief unidentified American diary of the
    siege of Yorktown, reprinted from the American
    Museum, Philadelphia, 1787.

11. Achenwall, Gottfried (1719-1772)

    "Achenwall's Observations on North America, 1767,"
    tr. by J. G. Rosengarten, Pennsylvania Magazine of
    History and Biography, XXVII (1903), 1-19. Published
    in 1769 at Frankfurt and 1777 at Helmstedt as Einige
    anmerkungen über Nord-Amerika und über dasige
    grosbrittannische colonien. Aus mündlichen nachrichten
    des Herrn. D. Franklins verfasst...

        After Benjamin Franklin's visit to the University
    of Gottingen, Professor Achenwall wrote down his own
    "observations" on North America as he had derived them
    from conversation with Franklin. His brief comments
    on Virginia are concerned with the system of government
    and economic conditions.

    Clark, Travels, I, #185

12. Anburey, Thomas

Travels through the Interior Parts of America. In a Series of Letters. By an Officer....London: Printed for W. Lane, 1789. 2 vols., plates, maps.

Lieutenant Anburey was captured at Saratoga and came to Charlottesville, Virginia, in January of 1779 as a prisoner of war. During his two-year residence there, he visited plantations in the Piedmont and along the James River to the southeast as far as Richmond. His account of his travels, written later, includes material from other sources, notably Burnaby and Smyth. (See Whitfield J. Bell, "Thomas Anburey's 'Travels through America': a Note on Eighteenth-Century Plagiarism," Papers of the Bibliographical Society of America, XXXVII (1943), 23-36.) His descriptions, however, are colorful. Though he approved of Virginia's class distinctions and deplored the leveling influence of the Revolution, he was as critical of the planter and his slaves as he was contemptuous of the middling sort.

Clark, Travels, I, #192

13. Asbury, Francis (1745-1816)

The Journal of the Rev. Francis Asbury, Bishop of the Methodist Episcopal Church, from August 7, 1771, to December 7, 1815....New York: N. Bangs and T. Mason, 1821. 3 vols.

In the period 1775-1783 "the Father of Methodism in America" paid several visits to Virginia, which, he declared, "pleases me in preference to all other places." In his work among the common people in the Southside and in the Valley, he preached against slavery and religious prejudice while organizing Methodist congregations. Though his journal records only routine religious activities, it reflects living conditions in the frontier communities where his most effective work was done. In December of 1782 he preached in the James City Courthouse--apparently to an unresponsive congregation, for he summarized

the "suffering" of the old capital thus: "the
worldly glory is departed from it--as to divine
glory it never had any."

Clark, Travels, II, #133

14.   Aston, Anthony (fl. 1682-1747)

"A Sketch of the Life of Anthony Aston, Written by
Himself," in Watson Nicholson, Anthony Aston Stroller
and Adventurer (South Haven, Mich.: Published by the
Author, 1920), pp. 51-63. Also in The Fool's Opera;
or, The Taste of the Age, Written by Mat Medley And
Performed by His Company in Oxford. London: T. Payne,
1731 (?).

     This famous wag, as well known in every town in
England "as the horse that carries the mail," visited
America in 1703-1704. He summarized his career and
travels: "Gentleman, Lawyer, Poet, Actor, Soldier,
Exciseman, Publican; in England, Scotland, Ireland,
New-York, East and West Jersey, Maryland, (Virginia
on both sides Cheesapeek,) North and South Carolina,
South Florida, Bahama's, Jamaica, Hispaniola, and
often a Coaster by all the same; like the Signs of the
Ablative Case...; for I been in 'em, travell'd through
'em, paid for 'em, come off genteely from 'em, and
liv'd by 'em." He stopped in Virginia briefly in the
fall of 1703 en route to New York, where he spent the
winter "acting, writing, courting, fighting." In the
spring he was again in Virginia as guest of Governor
Nicholson, who treated him "handsomely till the Fleet
under Commodore Evans" sailed for England.

Clark, Travels, I, #32

15.   Atkinson, Roger (1725-c.1784)

"Letters of Roger Atkinson, 1769-1776," Virginia
Magazine of History and Biography, XV (1908), 345-359.

     Atkinson came to Virginia from England about 1750
and became a planter at Mansfield, near Petersburg.

Most of these letters are to London merchants about the tobacco trade; the letter of August 25, 1772 to Lyonel and Samuel Lyde, pp. 352-354, describes the shift of tobacco culture from Tidewater to Piedmont and the growing importance of wheat in the Virginia economy. Two letters to his brother-in-law, Samuel Pleasants of Philadelphia, discuss public affairs in Virginia: in October 1774 he describes the Virginia delegates to the Continental Congress, and in November 1776 the Assembly then sitting in Williamsburg, "the People's men."

16. Baily, Francis (1774-1844)

Journal of a Tour in Unsettled Parts of North America, in 1796 & 1797. London: Baily Brothers, 1856. 439 p.

Baily landed at Norfolk in February 1796, then went on to Baltimore by boat and thence into the Mississippi Valley. He was never in Tidewater Virginia.

Clark, Travels, II, #74

17. Barbé-Marbois, Francois, Marquis de (1745-1837)

Our Revolutionary Forefathers: the Letters of Francois, Marquis de Barbé-Marbois during his Residence in the United States as Secretary of the French Legation, 1779-1785. Tr. and ed. by Eugene Parker Chase. New York: Duffield & Co., 1929. 225 p.

Barbé-Marbois came to the United States with the Chevalier de la Luzerne in 1779. The journal, in the form of letters to his fiancée, is generally friendly to Americans. But he came south only as far as Maryland, and in spite of his friendship with Washington, Madison, and Jefferson, he did not visit Virginia.

Clark, Travels, I, #194

18. Bayard, Ferdinand Marie (1768-c.1836)

Voyage dans l'intérieur des États-Unis, à Bath, Winchester, dans la Vallée de Shenandoha...pendant
l'été de 1791. Paris: Chez Cocheris, 1797. 336 p.
Selections in A. J. Morrison, ed., Travels in Virginia
in Revolutionary Times (Lynchburg: J. P. Bell Co.,
1922), pp. 81-89.

Although Bayard spent the entire summer in the
Valley, he did meet Tidewater Virginians; his sprightly
and detailed comments on local tastes in food, conversation and amusements therefore reflect social standards of more sophisticated persons than the backwoodsmen one might expect him to describe.

Clark, Travels, II, #77

19. Bedinger, Sergt. Henry (1753-1843)

Military journal, July 1775-June 1776, in Danske
Dandridge, Historic Shepherdstown (Charlottesville,
1910), pp. 97-144.

Sergeant Bedinger went directly from Shepherdstown to Boston, and his journal thereafter is concerned with activity in New England.

20. Beebe, Lewis (1749-1816)

MS Journal, 1776-1801. Historical Society of
Pennsylvania. 3 vols. Film Colonial Williamsburg.

Dr. Beebe was educated at Yale and was prac-
ticing medicine in Sheffield, Mass., when the
Revolution began. His army service is described in
the first volume of his journal, published as "Journal of a Physician on the Expedition against Canada,
1776," Pennsylvania Magazine of History and Biography, LIX (1935), 321-361.

After the war, Beebe was a physician in Vermont, first in Manchester, then in Arlington. In 1786 he accepted the invitation of the Congregational Church in Pawlet to become its pastor and was ordained the following year. But his ministry was marked by stormy controversies within his congregation and he was relieved of his charge and unfrocked in 1791, probably because of too liberal theological views, too freely expressed.

The second volume of his journal covers a year's residence in Maryland. Traveling through Queen Anne County in the fall of 1799, he arrived at the home of John Cox desperately ill with the ague. The Cox family nursed him back to health, and a large section of the journal is devoted to an essay in praise of the family and their way of life. From March to May, 1800, he was a tutor in the home of Mr. Pratt, "the heaviest man as to property in the County of Queen Anns." Dr. Beebe admired the elegance of the house (a "Palace") and the beauty of the garden (a "Paradise") and thoroughly enjoyed the luxuries of the table, but disapproved of the slavery, profanity, gambling and drinking all about him. He visited Washington in the summer, spent two days in Leesburg, and then returned to New England.

In Beebe's description of Maryland people and customs, there is a strong implication that he was drawing a picture of plantation life in Virginia as well: the plan of a formal garden (where flowers and vegetables were surrounded by avenues of fruit trees), farming methods, food, drink, manners, amusements, holidays.

21. Bernard, John (1756-1828)

Restrospections of America, 1797-1811, ed. by Mrs. Bayle Bernard....New York: Harper and Brothers, 1887. 380 p., illus.

This popular English actor spent the summer of 1799 in Virginia, where he enjoyed the amusements of plantation society, notably hunting and horse racing. In his reminiscences he commented favorably on the race course in Williamsburg (but did not locate or

describe it) and on the intelligence and breadth
of knowledge of Virginia gentlemen and the "refining"
influence of their wives. Bernard's style is con-
sciously literary, and in an effort to be amusing he
sometimes sacrificed truth in the interest of a good
story.

Clark, Travels, II, #3

22. Black, William

Travel diary, May-June, 1744, in Pennsylvania Magazine
of History and Biography, I (1877), 117-132, 233-249,
404-419; II (1888), 40-49.

Black was one of the Virginia commissioners who
signed the Lancaster Treaty with the Indians. His
sprightly diary records stops at Annapolis and Philadelphia, social activities along the way, and amusements to pass the time. Nothing of Tidewater Virginia.

23. Blanchard, Claude (1742-1802)

The Journal of Claude Blanchard, Commissary of the
French Auxiliary Army Sent to the United States during
the American Revolution, 1780-1783. Tr. by William
Duane, and ed. by Thomas Balch. Albany: J. Munsell,
1876. 207 p.

Contains a day-by-day account of Blanchard's
experiences as chief commissary to Rochambeau's army,
with emphasis on military maneuvers as they affected
his problems of supplies for the army and wounded.
During the Yorktown campaign and throughout the
following winter, his headquarters were in Williamsburg, which he described.

Clark, Travels, I, #201

24.   Boucher, Jonathan (1738-1806)

Reminiscences of an American Loyalist, 1738-1789;
Being the Autobiography of the Revd. Jonathan
Boucher, Rector of Annapolis in Maryland and after-
wards Vicar of Epsom, Surrey, England. Ed. by his
grandson Jonathan Bouchier. Boston: Houghton Mifflin
Co., 1925. 201 p.

    Boucher came to Virginia in 1759 to act as
tutor in the home of Captain Dixon, merchant at
Port Royal. After two years he took orders and
served parishes in King George and Caroline counties.
In the latter place he managed a plantation and a
boys' school for seven years; among his pupils were
John Parke Custis and James Madison (later Bishop
Madison, President of the College of William and
Mary, who was described by Boucher as "pert and
petulant").

    In 1770 he moved to Annapolis. By the time of
the Revolution his loyalist convictions and connec-
tions made him unacceptable to his patriot parishioners and neighbors, and he returned to England.

    His reminiscences about Virginia are too gen-
eral to be of great value to the historian of that
area; the story of the development of his loyalist
position in Maryland, however, has a wider application.

Clark, Travels, I, #202

25.   Bownas, Samuel (1676-1753)

An account of the Life, Travels, and Christian Ex-
periences in the Work of the Ministry of Samuel
Bownas. London: Printed by Luke Hinde, 1756. 198 p.
Reprinted in Friends' Library, III (1837), 1-70.

    This Westmoreland Quaker preacher made two
missionary journeys to America: one in 1702-1706, the
other in 1727-1728. On the second trip he came direct to Virginia, landing at Hampton. He held meetings
and conducted funerals in Nansemond and Surrey counties

and en route to Maryland paused on the Rappahannock
for a funeral. His badly organized account of his
travels is concerned almost entirely with doctrinal
matters; there are no comments on customs, even at
funerals, and the only characteristic of Virginia
people that interested him was their longevity,
which he attributed to the climate.

Clark, Travels, I, #41

26. Brandmueller, John. See MORAVIAN MISSIONARIES.

27. Brissot de Warville, Jacques Pierre (1754-1793)

New Travels in the United States of America. Performed in 1788. [Tr. by Joel Barlow]. New York:
Printed by T. & J. Swords, 1792. 262 p.

   Brissot traveled in the United States "to
study men who had just acquired their liberty,"
eager to prove to his countrymen that the American
experiment was a success which should be imitated
in France. His narrative, therefore, preaches a
great deal and points morals. He was especially
interested in Quakers and spent the greater part
of his time in America in Pennsylvania and New
England. He was in Virginia less than a week,
visiting Mount Vernon and Alexandria. Chapter 35
describes Mount Vernon. Chapter 36, "General Observations on Maryland and Virginia," is very general indeed, largely devoted to the degrading effects of slavery on master and slave alike. There
are short essays on the tobacco economy and tobacco
notes, which he ill understood, and on the Valley,
which he did not visit because the Revolution in
France called him home.

Clark, Travels, II, #80

28.   Brooke, Francis J.

"Virginia Campaign under Lafayette, 1781," <u>Magazine of History</u>, XXIII (1921), 9-30.

Personal narrative, written late in life.

29.   Brookes, Richard (fl. 1750)

<u>The General Gazetteer; or, Compendious Geographical Dictionary</u>...London: J. Newbery, 1762. 756 p., maps.

Dr. Brookes, though a compiler of geographical information, may be called a traveler because he wrote at the end of his article on Virginia: "And of this I am the more certain, because I have made it my business to enquire into, and examine these particulars on the spot." His <u>Gazetteer</u>, however, contains only the usual comments on the natural and economic geography of the colonies.

Clark, <u>Travels</u>, I, #205

30.   Brown, Tarleton (1757-1846)

<u>Memoirs of Tarleton Brown</u>, <u>A Captain of the Revolutionary Army</u>, <u>Written by Himself</u>. Preface and Notes by Charles I. Bushnell. New York: Privately printed, 1862. 65 p.

Brown, a native of Albemarle County, migrated with his family to South Carolina in 1769, and his reminiscences here published are entirely concerned with the war in the Carolinas.

Clark, <u>Travels</u>, I, #206

31.   Browne, Charlotte

"With Braddock's Army: Mrs. Browne's Diary in Virginia and Maryland," <u>Virginia Magazine of History and</u>

Biography, XXXII (1924), 305-320. Also in
Isabel Calder, Colonial Captivities (New York,
1935), pp. 169-200.

    The complete manuscript, in the Library of
Congress, is entitled "Journal of a Voyage from
London to Virginia, 1754." The author, a widow
who refers to herself as "Madam Browne," came to
America with her brother, a commissary officer in
Braddock's army. The Virginia part of her diary
includes sidelights on life in Alexandria--housing
difficulties, social attitudes of neighbors--and
on travel conditions in the trip from Alexandria
to Ft. Cumberland via Winchester--roads, weather,
inns, food, hospitality.

32.   Buchanan, Col. John

Journal, October 1745, in Goodridge Wilson, Smyth
County History and Traditions (n.p., 1932), pp. 10-15.

    The author, a semi-literate surveyor, records
data relative to land surveys and warrants on a trip
into southwest Virginia. There is only one extra-
neous entry in the journal--a curious conversation
with a Dunker bachelor about marriage: Colonel
Buchanan was of the opinion that sex came with Adam's
fall, that in Eden man propagated his species without
the assistance of woman.

33.   Burnaby, Rev. Andrew (1734?-1812)

Travels through the Middle Settlements in North-America,
in the Years 1759 and 1760. 2nd ed., London: T. Payne,
1775. 198 p. with table, "Diary of the weather," Jan-
uary-December 1760, transmitted from Williamsburg by
Governor Fauquier. Extracts in Virginia Historical
Register, V (1852), 27-38, 81-93, 144-157.

    Burnaby came to Virginia from England in July 1759
and remained here until June 1760, leaving only four
months for a trip from Maryland to New Hampshire; he

therefore understood Virginia better than the other
colonies, and the best part of his book is devoted
to that colony. He was an accurate observer of geography, government, economy and religion, and his
comments on the character of the people and their
social life and customs are among the most penetrating to be found in the observations of foreign travelers.

Clark, Travels, II, #7

34. Burnham, Major John

"Personal Recollections of the Revolutionary War,"
Magazine of History, XIX (1917), 110-133. Reprinted
Tarrytown: W. Abbatt, 1917.

    Burnham was a major in the Massachusetts Con-
tinental Line. His reminiscences include brief
descriptive material on the siege of Yorktown and
anecdotes of General Steuben.

35. Burr, Isaac

Travel diary, September-November 1805, in Journal
of American History, III (1909), 447-452.

    On a trip from New York through western Penn-
sylvania and the Valley of Virginia to Abingdon,
Burr itemized his expenses and made interesting
comments on the lives of the "middling sort." He
did not come into Tidewater Virginia, however.

36. Butler, Richard

"General Richard Butler's Journal of the Siege of
Yorktown," Historical Magazine, VIII (1864), 102-112.

    Day-by-day account of the Yorktown campaign, Sep-
tember 1-October 25, 1781, by a colonel in Wayne's
Pennsylvania brigade. One of the best personal accounts
of the siege.

37.   Büttner, Johann Carl (b. 1754)

Narrative of Johann Carl Büttner in the American
Revolution. New York: Printed for C. F. Heartman,
1915. 69 p.

      An indentured servant to a New Jersey Quaker,
Büttner joined Major von Ortendorff's corps of
German volunteers, then deserted to the Hessians.
He never came to Virginia.

Clark, Travels, I, #207

38.   Byrd, William (1674-1744)

John Spencer Bassett, ed., The Writings of "Colonel
William Byrd, of Westover in Virginia, Esqr." New
York: Doubleday, Page & Co., 1901. 461 p.

The Secret Diary of William Byrd of Westover, 1709-
1712. Ed. by Louis B. Wright and Marion Tinling.
Richmond: Dietz Press, 1941. 622 p.

Another Secret Diary of William Byrd of Westover,
1739-1741, With Letters & Literary Exercises, 1696-
1726. Ed. by Maude H. Woodfin, tr. and collated by
Marion Tinling. Richmond: Dietz Press, 1942. 490 p.

The London Diary (1717-1721) and Other Writings. Ed.
by Louis B. Wright and Marion Tinling. New York:
Oxford Univ. Press, 1958. 647 p.

      While Byrd was a resident of Tidewater Virginia,
he was one of our most confirmed travelers at home as
well as abroad. His letters and formal writings reflect his prominent position in Virginia life and
politics, his engaging personality and cultural pol-
ish, and establish his qualifications as an inter-
preter of the society of which he was the chief
ornament. His secret diaries are unique as historical source material because they record completely
frank opinions, uninhibited by any thought of their
being read by any other human being.

Clark, Travels, I, #48-50

39. Cadignan, Chevalier Dupleix de

Extract from the Journal of Chevalier Dupleix de
Cadignan, Lieutenant-Colonel in the Agenois Regiment during the War for American Independence
at the Siege of Yorktown. Translated from the
French by Warrington Dawson. Dawson Papers, Colonial Williamsburg, Memorandum No. 26, New Series,
enclosure. The full MS is in the Chateau de la
Garde, Montreal-du-Gers, Gers Department, France.

   This fragment of Cadignan's journal describes
Williamsburg as the French army saw it in 1781, the
march to Yorktown and the opening moves of the siege.

40. Calk, William

Travel diary, March-May 1775, in <u>Mississippi Valley
Historical Review</u>, VII (1920-21), 363-377.

   A planter-merchant in Prince William County,
Calk recorded in this diary a trip to Boone's Fort,
Kentucky, and back.

41. Carew, Bampfylde Moore (1693-1758)

<u>The Life and Adventures of Bampfylde-Moore Carew,
the Noted Devonshire Stroller and Dog-stealer; as
Related by Himself, during His Passage to the
Plantations in America</u>. <u>Containing a Great Variety
of Remarkable Transactions in a Vagrant Course of
Life</u>...Exon [Exeter]: Printed by the Farleys for
Joseph Drew, 1745, 152 p.

   This volume is a literary curiosity with no
historical value, though it has gone through more
than forty editions. The "King of the Beggars" came
to America probably in the 1730's (no date is given
in the autobiography). He landed at Hampton, then
went to Talbot County, Md. He later returned to
Virginia, he says, to live for a time by begging.

Clark, <u>Travels</u>, I, #52

42. Carter, Landon (1710-1778)

MS Diary, 1763-1778, in Sabine Hall Papers, Alderman Library; selections printed in William and Mary Quarterly, 1st ser., XIV-XXI.

MS Plantation Diary, 1751-58, 1772-77, privately owned but now on deposit in Alderman Library.

MS Almanac Diary, 1766-67, William L. Clements Library; copy at Alderman Library and Colonial Williamsburg.

When used in connection with the personal papers in the Sabine Hall collection, these diaries furnish excellent source material on the political history of the Revolution in Virginia and on agricultural practices, as well as Carter himself--planter, patriot, scientist, philosopher, and eccentric. The diaries are included in this bibliography because their author visited Williamsburg regularly while he was a Burgess from Richmond County (1748-1764), and the Plantation Diary in particular contains references to life here during Public Times and an especially useful description of procedure in the House of Burgesses.

43. Carter, Robert (1663-1732)

MS Diary, 1722-1728. Alderman Library.

Seven letterbooks, 1723-1732, four in the Alderman Library and three in the Virginia Historical Society.

Letters of Robert Carter, 1720-1727..., ed. by Louis B. Wright. San Marino: Huntington Library, 1940. 153 p. (This is the one letterbook owned by the Huntington Library, together with a few other manuscripts relating to Carter's estate.)

Since "King" Carter was the most successful business man in colonial Virginia, his personal papers are of great value to students of the Virginia economy at the beginning of the 18th century. Like his son Landon, he was a frequent visitor in Williamsburg. As a member (and President) of the Council and member of the Board of Visitors (and Rector) of the College of William and Mary, he attended to public business here; as agent for the Proprietors of the Northern Neck, to land business. Fortunately, the diary covers the year of his governorship (1726-1727).

The papers have been badly damaged by dampness and vermin and are hard to read, but the diary and letterbooks owned by the Alderman Library and the Virginia Historical Society are scheduled for publication by the Society.

44. Carver, Jonathan (1710-1780)

Travels through the Interior Parts of North-America, in the Years 1766, 1767, and 1768. London: Printed for the Author, 1778. 543 p.

This book is largely concerned with Indian life and customs, plants and animals in the Northwest. Carver probably never came to Virginia.

45. Castiglioni, Luigi (1756-1832)

Viaggio negli State Uniti dell' America Settentrionale, fatto negli anni 1785, 1786, e 1787...Milan: Stamperia di G. Marelli, 1790. 2 vols.

Too gazetteer-ish to be of much value; Count Castiglioni probably copied extensively from other travelers. The Virginia part of the tour is given in Vol. I, Chap. 11, pp. 349-391, organized as follows: the Shenandoah Valley; geographical features of the state as a whole; contemporary Virginia, its form of government, cities, plantation economy, and variety of beverages; Kentucky.

Clark, Travels, II, #84

46.   Catesby, Mark (1682-1749)

The Natural History of Carolina, Florida and the
Bahama Islands...London: Printed for the Author,
1731-1743. 2 vols.

     Catesby's extended visit in the home of his
sister, Mrs. William Cocke, from 1712 to 1719 is
beautifully recorded in the drawings of plants and
animals that charmed him here as well as in the
area to the south of us. But his travel narrative
is restricted to the southern trip of 1722, which
dictated the title of his book.

Clark, Travels, I, #55

47.   Chalkley, Thomas (1675-1741)

A Journal or Historical Account of the Life, Travels,
and Christian Experiences of that Antient, Faithful
Servant of Jesus Christ, Thomas Chalkley...2nd ed.
London: Luke Hinde, 1751. 326 p. Reprinted in
Friends' Library, VI (1842), 1-176.

     Useful only to a biographer of Chalkley, Quaker
missionary from Philadelphia who visited Virginia
congregations but recorded nothing of the people who
composed them. The journal reflects the author's
personal piety and hatred of Anglicans and Presbyterians, but there is no evidence that his congregations
shared his prejudices.

Clark, Travels, I, #56

48.   Chastellux, Francois Jean, Marquis de (1734-1788)

Travels in North-America, in the Years 1780, 1781, and
1782. Tr. from the French by an English Gentleman...
With Notes by the Translator. London: G. G. J. & J.
Robinson, 1787. 2 vols. A recent and much better
edition is translated with introduction, notes, maps,
illustrations by Howard C. Rice, Jr. Chapel Hill:
Published for the Institute of Early American History
and Culture by the Univ. of North Carolina Press, 1963.
2 vols.

Though one of Rochambeau's general officers at
Yorktown, Chastellux has little to say about military
affairs. After the war he visited Pennsylvania and
New England but spent the greater part of his travel
time in Virginia, where he went from Yorktown west to
Monticello, then up the Shenandoah Valley as far as
Natural Bridge and back in a circle to Williamsburg
via Southside Virginia to Petersburg then across the
James River and down the north bank. Volume II of his
Travels is devoted to observations on Virginia, its
natural features and its people. While there is some
information on the economy and political organization
of the state and on travel conditions, his emphasis
is largely on Virginians of all classes, and their
manner of living, ideas and ideals. Chastellux was
an extravagant admirer of Jefferson because their
tastes were similar, and his breadth of interest and
philosophical approach to his subject made him an unusually perceptive observer. Moreover, his great
personal charm gave him a warm reception everywhere
he went, and he knew the people he described. Alto-
gether, his Travels is one of the most valuable
sources for the social historian.

Clark, Travels, I, #212

49. Churchman, John (1705-1775)

An Account of the Gospel Labours, and Christian
Experiences of a Faithful Minister of Christ, John
Churchman...Philadelphia: Printed by Joseph Crukshank,
1779. 256 p. Reprinted in Friends' Library, VI (1842),
176-267.

Churchman was a Pennsylvania Quaker more typical
of his sect than Chalkley, a preacher of love more
than hate, but no more interesting to the historian.
He visited congregations and individuals in Virginia
in 1740, 1759 and 1760, holding meetings in the
Shenandoah, at Fairfax and Goose Creek.

Clark, Travels, I, #64

50.   Clarke, George (1676-1760)

Voyage of George Clarke, Esq., to America. With
Introduction and Notes, by E. B. O'Callaghan. Albany:
J. Munsell, 1867. 126 p.

        A nephew of William Blathwayt, Clarke came to
New York in 1703 to act as provincial secretary.
The voyage and the narrative began in London in
April and ended in July, when the ship cast anchor
"in Virginia."

Clark, Travels, I, #65

51.   Clinton, Sir Henry (1738?-1795)

Narrative of Lieutenant-General Sir Henry Clinton,
K.B. Relative to his Conduct during Part of his
Command of the King's Troops in North America....
London: Printed for J. Debrett, 1783. 87 p.

        Clinton's justification of his part in the cam-
paign culminating at Yorktown. The appearance of
this pamphlet marked the beginning of a public con-
troversy with Cornwallis. (The series of pamphlets
exchanged by Clinton and Cornwallis, with those of
their partisans, were reprinted in Benjamin Franklin
Stevens, The Campaign of Virginia, 1781, 2 vols.
London, 1888).

        See also The American Rebellion: Sir Henry
Clinton's Narrative of His Campaigns, 1775-1782,
with an Appendix of Original Documents. Ed. by
William B. Willcox. New Haven: Yale Univ. Press,
1954. 658 p., maps.

52.   Closen, Jean Christophe Louis Frederic Ignace,
       Baron von (1752?-1830)

Revolutionary Journal, 1780-1783. Tr. and ed. with
an introd. by Evelyn M. Acomb. Chapel Hill: Published
for the Institute of Early American History and Culture
by the Univ. of N. C. Press, 1958. 392 p., illus.,
ports., map.

Von Closen was a captain in the Deux-Ponts
Regiment when they came to America, an intelligent
and conscientious officer. He demonstrated unusual
courage under fire at Yorktown and acted as inter-
preter in conferences between Washington and
Rochambeau. His journal of the campaign is one of
the most informative contemporary records.

He was a good reporter of non-military affairs
also, for his intellectual curiosity led him to
study American politics, economy and social institutions; furthermore his good disposition and sense
of humor add charm to his descriptions and comments.
His ideas of Virginia geography remained somewhat
hazy; otherwise his reporting is accurate in detail.
His journal is excellent for travel conditions immediately after the war--roads, inn accommodations,
sites connected with the history of the Revolution.
He was stationed in Williamsburg long enough to
describe the town and people with unusual insight.
In February 1782 he accompanied Rochambeau on a
trip to the West, visiting a number of James River
plantations en route. Von Closen's descriptions of
Offly-Hoo, Scotchtown, Tuckahoe, Westover, Monticello
and Mount Vernon are especially interesting because
they include the hosts as well as the estates.

53. [Cluny, Alexander]

The American Traveller: or, Observations on the
Present State, Culture and Commerce of the British
Colonies in America....In a series of Letters Writ-
ten Originally to the Right Honourable the Earl of
---. By an Old and Experienced Trader. London:
Printed for E. and C. Dilly, 1769. 122 p., world
map.

Letter XVI describes Virginia and Maryland together
because they were "in all Respects circumstanced so ex-
actly alike by Nature, and so inexplicably connected
with each other in Trade and Intercourse." The essay
is entirely devoted to commerce; it lists commodities
exported from England to the two colonies and from
Maryland and Virginia to England and other markets,

explains how the balance of trade was against
England, and examines the evils of the tobacco
trade.

Clark, Travels, I, #213

54. Cobb, Lieutenant-Colonel David

"Before Yorktown, Virginia, October 1-November 30,
1781," Massachusetts Historical Society Proceedings,
XIX (1881-1882), 67-75.

     Cobb was an aide-de-camp to Washington during
the Yorktown campaign. Brief diary followed by a
letter summing up the campaign.

55. Coke, Thomas (1747-1814)

Extracts of the Journals of the Rev. Dr. Coke's Five
Visits to America. London: Printed by G. Paramore
and sold by G. Whitefield, 1793. 195 p.

     This Methodist missionary made nine visits to
America; journals of six of them have survived. (See
Clark, Travels, II, #85 for details of their bibliography and for Coke's "meanderings" in the United States.)
He visited Virginia on at least five of the journeys,
sometimes accompanied by Asbury, but he was never in
Tidewater Virginia below Richmond and Alexandria. His
journals contain no description of local conditions
and reveal little of his missionary activities. We
do learn from them that he preached against slavery
and presented antislavery petitions to Washington and
to the Virginia Assembly.

56. Contenson, Ludovic de, ed.

"Deux Documents sur la Guerre d'Amérique," Revue
d'Histoire Diplomatique, XLIV (1930), 20-34.

Introductory material and two documents: (1) a
letter of Baron de Verton, a lieutenant of the Auxonne
artillery regiment, explaining the decisive part
played by the artillery in the siege of Yorktown;
(2) the latter part of Saint-Simon's journal, covering the events in the West Indies after Yorktown,
through de Grasse's defeat and capture in April, 1782.

57. Contenson, Ludovic de, ed.

"La Capitulation de Yorktown et le Comte de Grasse,"
Revue d'Histoire Diplomatique, XLII (1928), 378-399.

The title is misleading. This is an edition of
that part of the journal of the Marquis de Saint-Simon
covering the Yorktown campaign, including events in
the West Indies in 1781 and the voyage to the Chesapeake of de Grasse's fleet. Saint-Simon commanded
the French brigade brought to Virginia with the fleet.

58. Cresswell, Nicholas (1750-1804)

The Journal of Nicholas Cresswell, 1774-1777. New
York: The Dial Press, 1924. 287 p. MS Colonial
Williamsburg.

Cresswell came to America seeking his fortune,
but the time was ill chosen for a loyalist and he
spent three years in frustrated ideleness and per-
iodic drunkenness--all regretted. In May 1774 he
landed at Urbanna bound for Alexandria, the home of
his prospective guide and patron, Mr. Kirk. As his
American headquarters he used Kirk's business es-
tablishments in Alexandria and Leesburg, with trips
into Maryland, the Valley, New York, and finally
Williamsburg on the way home. His journal is most
valuable for comments on the growth of the revolutionary movement in Virginia with an accompanying
picture of his own position as a suspected Tory:
he reports news from other sections of Virginia
and from other colonies as well as local fast days,
musters, military reviews, political and military
activity. Since he found Virginia "the finest

country I ever was in" and wanted to buy a farm
in Frederick County, his observations about farming methods are more detailed than the usual traveler's; they include tobacco planting and cultiva-
tion (pp. 17-18), wheat harvesting (p. 55), milling
(at Washington's mill, pp. 26-27), an estimate of
the costs and profits of such a farm (pp. 195-199),
a summary of Virginia's natural resources and economy (pp. 266-268). On pp. 130-131 is a detailed
description of Continental currency, with mottoes
and designs of each denomination. He was interested,
too, in social customs and described holidays, balls,
barbecues, a reaping frolic (or harvest festival), a
Negro ball, and informal amusements. His portrayal
of George Washington is a moving tribute because his
admiration was so reluctantly given.

Clark, Travels, I, #217

59. Crèvecoeur, Michel Guillaume St. Jean de (1735-1813)

Letters from an American Farmer....London: Printed for
Thomas Davies..., 1782. 318 p.

None of the letters deals with Virginia.

Clark, Travels, I, #218

60. Cromot du Bourg, Marie Francois Joseph Maxime, Baron

"Diary of a French Officer 1781 (Presumed to be that
of Baron Cromot du Bourg, Aide to Rochambeau),"
Magazine of American History, IV (1880), 205-214,
293-308, 376-385, 441-449; VII (1881), 283-295.

Journal kept by a French officer with Rochambeau's
army, who arrived in Williamsburg September 18, dined
with Lafayette, and spent the 20th and 21st sight-seeing, visiting Queen's Creek and College Landing.

61. Cunningham, Adam (fl. 1730)

Whitfield J. Bell, Jr., ed., "Adam Cunningham's
Atlantic Crossing, 1728," Maryland Historical Mag-
azine, L (1955), 195-202. Manuscripts owned by
Mrs. Dick-Cunnyngham and Mrs. Janet Oliver of
Prestonfield, Edinburgh; transcripts Colonial
Williamsburg.

This young Scot came to Virginia planning to
establish a medical practice. His journal of the
voyage presents a vivid picture of the hardships
and dangers of the trip, which "continued 6 months
and 17 days." The journal closes with his arrival
in Hampton Roads, but two subsequent letters to his
father describe conditions in the practice of
medicine in Williamsburg and in King George County.

62. D'Ancteville, Chevalier

Campagne de la Chesapeake (Journal of the Chesapeake
Campaign). MS in Archives Nationales, Marine B4 184,
folio 145 to 157; transcript prepared for Warrington
Dawson in 1931 and copy furnished to Colonial National
Historical Park. Printed in part in William and Mary
Quarterly, 2nd ser., XX (1940), 502-503, and Legion
d'Honneur, II, No. 2 (Yorktown Number, October, 1931),
83-96.

One of the most detailed and precise of the personal documents covering the Yorktown campaign; it
describes Lafayette's army and the town of Williamsburg. The author was a French engineer serving with
Saint-Simon's brigade, which came from the West Indies
on board de Grasse's fleet.

63. Davis, John (1774-1854)

Travels of Four Years and a Half in the United States
of America during 1798, 1799, 1800, 1801, and 1802.
London: Sold by T. Ostell and T. Hurst, 1803. 454 p.

Davis came to America in search of literary employment. Armed with letters of introduction from Burr and Jefferson, he traveled from New York to Georgia, back and forth several times. In Virginia he was twice a tutor: for three months in a Quaker family on the Occoquan and for another three months at Pohoke, a Ball plantation near Newgate, Prince William County. He did not visit Williamsburg.

His travel account was written shortly after the events related--possibly from diary notes, but also from other accounts--and its value to the historian is further lessened by his frequent sur-render to the temptation to spin a good yarn. In his description of his "academy" at Pohoke (an old field school) and the sketchy account of his tutor-ial duties there, he is in no way comparable to Fithian; but he was a strong advocate of literary education for women, and his attention to the girl students' reading provides a supplement to the Nomini Hall curriculum. His sketch of plantation family life is more nearly typical than Fithian's, for he served "small" planters. Davis was more sophisticated than Fithian and better humored, but he was equally critical of the institution of slavery, and his re-telling of the life story of Dick, an old slave at Pohoke, is somewhat sentimental. On pp. 305 ff. there is a description of a service at Pohick Church, with Parson Weems in the pulpit.

Clark, Travels, II, #86

64. Davis, Capt. John

"Diary of Capt. John Davis, of the Pennsylvania Line," Virginia Magazine of History and Biography, I (1893), 1-16. Also in Pennsylvania Magazine of History and Biography, V (1881), 290-305, with minor variations in the text.

A journal of the Virginia campaign of 1781 cover-ing the movements of Wayne's force from May 26 to the departure of the Pennsylvania Line for South Carolina after Yorktown. Military only.

65. Dearborn, Henry (1751-1829)

Revolutionary War Journals of Henry Dearborn,
1775-1783, edited from the Original Manuscripts by
Lloyd A. Brown and Howard H. Peckham; with a Biographical Essay by Hermon Dunlap Smith. Chicago:
The Caxton Club, 1939. 264 p. Also in Massachusetts
Historical Society Proceedings, 2d. ser., III (1888),
103-133.

        The journals are largely concerned with
Dearborn's personal military record, with less
detail about the problems of sanitation and care
of the wounded than one would expect from his interest in medicine. His description of the Virginia
campaign of 1781 is brief and factual, with comments
on illness within the British lines at Yorktown.

Clark, Travels, I, #219

66. Denny, Ebenezer (1761-1822)

Military Journal of Major Ebenezer Denny...with an
Introductory Memoir [by W. H. Denny]. Philadelphia:
Historical Society of Pennsylvania, 1859. 288 p.
Also in Historical Society of Pennsylvania Memoirs,
VII (1860), 205-492.

        A native of Carlisle, Pennsylvania, Denny came
South with Wayne, fought with Lafayette at Richmond
and with Simcoe at Williamsburg and Yorktown. A
factual account of immediate events, a good military
journal, with brief descriptions of Williamsburg, of
the camp behind the College, and of exercises and
parades (Sept. 1-28). Good detail on the siege of
Yorktown.

Clark, Travels, II, #18

67. Deux-Ponts, Count William de (1745-   )

My Campaigns in America: A Journal kept by Count
William de Deux-Ponts, 1780-81. Tr. from the French

manuscript, with an introd. and notes by Samuel
Abbott Green. Boston: J. K. Wiggin and Wm. Parsons
Lunt, 1868. 176 p.

One of the fullest and best of the French diaries covering the siege of Yorktown. Deux-Ponts,
who came to America in Rochambeau's army, led the
attack on Redoubt No. 9, October 14, 1781.

Clark, Travels, I, #223

68. Devereux, John William

Travel diary, June-November, 1799, in Georgia
Historical Quarterly, XV (1931), 46-80.

Devereux traveled from Milledgeville, Georgia,
to New York by sea, without stopping at a Virginia
port.

69. Dickinson, James

A Journal of the Life, Travels, and Labour of Love
in the Work of the Ministry, of That Worthy Elder,
and Faithful Servant of Jesus Christ, James Dickinson.
London: T. Sowle Raylton and Luke Hinde, 1745. 172 p.

This English Quaker made three missionary journeys to the American colonies--two in the 1690's, the
third in 1714. His journal records his work among
the lower classes but is concerned with little beyond
their spiritual welfare.

Clark, Travels, I, #72

70. Doehla, Johann Conrad (1750-1820)

Tagebuch eines Bayreuther Soldaten...aus dem
Nordamerikanischen Freiheitskrieg von 1777 bis 1785.
Bayreuth: Privately printed, 1913. 241 p., map. His

account of the year 1781, tr. by Robert J. Tilden,
was printed in <u>William and Mary Quarterly</u>, 2d ser.,
XXII (1942), 229-274, as "The Doehla Journal."

    A vivid and intimate picture of the Yorktown
campaign, seen through the eyes of a German merce-
nary soldier in the ranks. His information is
often inaccurate, but what he believed has signifi-
cance. His comments on non-military affairs in
Tidewater Virginia include descriptions of the
James River area, Norfolk, Fredericksburg, Yorktown and Williamsburg; his impressions of the
Virginia people; sand crabbing; Virginia cotton
culture.

Clark, <u>Travels</u>, I, #224

71. [Dornberg, Karl Ludwig, 1749-1819]

<u>Tagebuchblatter eines Hessischen Offiziers aus der
Zeit des Nordamerikanischen unabhangigkeits krieges</u>....
Pyritz, 1899-1900. 2 vols.

    No Virginia service.

Clark, <u>Travels</u>, I, #225

72. Douglass, William (1691-1752)

<u>A Summary, Historical and Political, of the First
Planting, Progressive Improvements and Present State
of the British Settlements in North-America</u>....Boston:
Printed by Rogers and Fowle, 1749-1752. 2 vols. (Map
in 1760 ed.)

    Since Dr. Douglass lived in Boston, his emphasis
is on New England. His section on Virginia, II, 385-416,
is an incomplete historical essay beginning with Columbus
and going to the Culpeper grant, then digressing into a
long descriptive history of smallpox in New England.
(An epidemic in Boston at the time of his writing closed
his printer's office.)

Clark, <u>Travels</u>, I, #226

73. Dumas, Count Mathieu (1753-1807)

   Memoirs of his own Time: including the Revolution,
   the Empire, and the Restoration. London: R. Bentley,
   1839. 2 vols.

      Largely devoted to the French Revolution and
   Napoleonic wars, but the early chapters of Vol. I
   include reminiscences of service with the French
   army in the American Revolution. There is some
   colorful detail on the siege of Yorktown, though
   Dumas draws frankly from Rochambeau's Memoirs in
   his narrative of the campaign. The Virginia part
   of the account ends with the winter of 1781 in
   Williamsburg quarters. Military only.

   Clark, Travels, I, #227

74. Duncan, Captain James

   "Diary of Captain James Duncan, of Colonel Moses
   Hazen's Regiment, in the Yorktown Campaign, 1781,"
   Pennsylvania Archives, 2nd ser., XV (1890), 743-752.

      Detailed journal of the siege of Yorktown al-
   though it covers only the period October 2-15, 1781.

75. Du Roi, August Wilhelm

   Journal of Du Roi the Elder, Lieutenant and Adjutant,
   in the Service of the Duke of Brunswick, 1776-1778.
   Tr. by Charlotte S. J. Epping. Philadelphia: Univ.
   of Pennsylvania, 1911. 189 p.

      Du Roi was captured at Saratoga and came to
   Virginia ahead of the other prisoners because he was
   von Riedesel's commissary of the Second Division. The
   Virginia part of his journal contains descriptions of
   Leesburg, Charlottesville and the nearby Hessian bar-
   racks, roads and travel conditions, and Piedmont soci-
   ety. It ends abruptly in March 1779, when he was in
   Richmond and planning to visit Williamsburg.

Du Roi found Virginia gentlemen sociable, courteous, lazy, and given to gambling; the lower class grasping and likely to impose on strangers; women more industrious than men.

Clark, Travels, I, #228

76. Eddis, William

Letters from America, Historical and Descriptive; Comprising Occurrences from 1769, to 1777, inclusive. London: Printed for the Author, 1792. 455 p.

In August 1769 Eddis stopped briefly at Yorktown en route to Annapolis, where as Governor Eden's secretary he came to know Maryland planters and officials. His essays on Southern society, speech, fashions, ladies, marriage customs, holidays and amusements are applicable to Virginia as well as Maryland. See Letter VI on servitude; Letter IX on amusements; Letter XX re. the Powder Magazine at Williamsburg; Letter XXVI re. Dunmore's emancipation proclamation, battle of Great Bridge, devastation of Norfolk, position of Virginia loyalists; Letter XXIX re. May 15, 1776 in Williamsburg.

Clark, Travels, I, #229

77. Evans, Lewis (c. 1700-1756)

Geographical, Historical, Political, Philosophical and Mechanical Essays. The First, Containing An Analysis of A General Map of the Middle British Colonies in America...Philadelphia: Printed by B. Franklin and D. Hall, 1755. 32 p., map.

This Evans map was used by Braddock. The essays that accompany it are short and largely geographical, with emphasis on the Ohio area, suggested portages and roads leading to the West.

Clark, Travels, I, #232

78. [Evans, Chaplain]

"Journal of the Siege of York in Virginia by a Chaplain of the American Army," Massachusetts Historical
Society Collections, 1st ser., IX (1804), 102-108.

Daily entries from September 12, 1781 (leaving
Head of Elk with the American army) to October 22
(a visit to Yorktown following the surrender). Precise and interesting military detail, with a brief
description of Williamsburg.

79. Ewald, J. von

Belehrungen uber den krief, besonders uber den
kleinen Krieg, durch Beispiele grosser Helden und
kluger und tapferen Manner. Schleswig, 1800.

In this military textbook Ewald draws freely
from his recollections of service with the army of
Cornwallis in the Carolinas and Virginia.

80. Fairfax, Sally Cary

"Diary of a Little Colonial Girl," Virginia Magazine of History and Biography, XI (1903-1904), 212-214.

The writer was a daughter of Bryan Fairfax of
Toulston, Fairfax County, a life-long friend of
George Washington and son of William Fairfax of
Belvoir. Sally's diary has survived only as a fragment for the period December 26, 1771 to February 14,
1772, and there is one letter to her father written
some years later, about 1778, when he was in New York
planning to go to England. The diary gives unusual
glimpses of plantation life, things of interest to a
little girl: parties, guests, food, new clothes, visits,
births and deaths of animals, her personal finances.
There is only one reference to the Revolution: "Mama
made some tea for a wonder indeed."

81. Feltman, William

The Journal of Lieut. William Feltman, of the First
Pennsylvania Regiment, 1781-82. Including the March
into Virginia and the Siege of Yorktown. Philadelphia:
Historical Society of Pennsylvania, 1853. 48 p. Also
in Historical Society of Pennsylvania Collections, I
(1853), 303-348, and Pennsylvania Archives, 2nd Ser.,
XI, 709-762.

     A good personal, military journal. Feltman
served with Wayne's Pennsylvania brigade throughout
the Virginia campaign and the subsequent march through
the Carolinas. On the march from Richmond, he noticed
by the roadside women "muffled up with linens" to
prevent sunburn, accompanied by naked Negro slaves.
He camped near Westover, at Jamestown and Green Spring,
at Nathaniel Burwell's mill (where he saw rice growing),
and finally at Williamsburg (where he was quartered on
the College Campus). He described the town briefly
and noted that Dr. Nicholson entertained a number of
Pennsylvanians with "a good dinner, a glass of spirits
and Madeira wine." On September 14 he "mounted the
Centre Picquet near the wind-mill, in Williamsburg"
and on the 17th went crabbing at College Landing.

82. Finlay, Hugh

Journal Kept by Hugh Finlay, Surveyor of the Post Roads
on the Continent of North America, during his Survey
of the Post Offices between Falmouth and Casco Bay, in
the Province of Massachusetts, and Savannah in Georgia;
Begun the 13th Sept. 1773 and Ended 26th June 1774.
Brooklyn: Frank H. Norton, 1867. 94 p., maps.

     When Finlay succeeded Franklin as surveyor of
post roads and post offices, he inspected both Northern
and Southern districts and recorded conditions of post
offices and roads, routes, and schedules of post riders
and others who carried the mails, violations of regu-
lations, and suggestions for improving the service.
In Virginia he visited Suffolk (the most southern town
in the Northern District and the transfer point for

mail from each direction), Norfolk, Hampton, and
Yorktown, but not Williamsburg.

Clark, Travels, I, #238

83. Fisher, Daniel

Journal, 1750-1755, "The Fisher History," in Louise
Pecquet du Bellet, Some Prominent Virginia Families
(Lynchburg: J. P. Bell, 1907), II, 752-812. Printed
in part as "Narrative of George Fisher," William and
Mary Quarterly, 1st ser., XVII (1908-1909), 100-139,
147-176.

One of the most useful sources of information
about Williamsburg ordinaries and innkeepers. Fisher
had been in Virginia in 1722 and returned three decades later planning to go into business. The first
part of his journal gives a detailed account of the
trip from London to Yorktown: arranging passage,
supplies and introductions; the voyage itself, when
he received special attention after his successful
treatment of a case of smallpox on board. From
September 1751 to May 1755 he was in Williamsburg,
where he rented the English Coffee House (Marot's)
from Wetherburn and kept an ordinary for four months,
then sublet tenements and kept a store in one apart-
ment. But he quarreled with everyone he met in
Yorktown and Jamestown--except Walthoe--and blaming
his "enemies" for his financial failures went on to
Philadelphia in search of better business opportunities. His journal is especially valuable to
Williamsburg historical research for lists of mer-
chandise, a detailed account of the Palmer House fire
of April 24, 1754, and references to Thomas and William Nelson, Nathaniel Walthoe, Henry Wetherburn,
Benjamin Waller, John Holt, John Blair, John Greenhow
and Philip Ludwell Lee.

84. Fithian, Philip Vickers (1747-1776)

Journal and Letters of Philip Vickers Fithian, 1773-1774:
A Plantation Tutor of the Old Dominion. Ed. by Hunter
Dickinson Farish. Williamsburg: Colonial Williamsburg,
Inc., 1943. 323 p., illus.

The best and fullest diary record we have of
life on a Virginia plantation. Since almost everything at Nomini Hall was different from what Fithian
was accustomed to at home in New Jersey, he described
his impressions of the plantation itself, the Carter
family and servants, Carter's business methods, social
life in the Northern Neck, all the people he met there.

For an analysis of Fithian's other published
papers, see Clark, Travels, I, #239, 240. The complete collection of his extant manuscripts is at
Princeton.

85. Fontaine, John

"Journal" in Ann Maury, ed., Memoirs of a Huguenot
Family: Translated and Compiled from the Original
Autobiography of the Rev. James Fontaine, and Other
Family Manuscripts....(New York: George P. Putnam &
Co., 1853), pp. 245-310.

Before he came to America, John Fontaine was an
ensign in Lord Shaw's Regiment in Spain. He arrived
in the Potomac in May 1715, then came to Williamsburg,
which he used as headquarters for several Virginia
tours: In November 1715 he went to Germantown, stopping along the way to visit Robert Beverley. The
following spring he went with Governor Spotswood and
others on a ten-day trip to Christianna and the
Saponey Indian town. From August 20 to September 17
the Knights of the Golden Horseshoe made their famous
transmontane expedition, recorded more fully by Fontaine
than by any other participant. He bought a plantation
in King William County, which he left in the hands of
two brothers and a brother-in-law when he "went home"
in 1719. The journal ends with his arrival in England.

If Fontaine kept a journal while he was in Williamsburg, the editor did not publish that part of it,
and so there is almost nothing about the town in it.
He did describe Yorktown and Hampton, and the journal
is good source material for life in Tidewater Virginia--
travel conditions (food, lodging, roads and ferries),
hospitality of the planters, Indian life. When Fontaine
was in New York, he usually went to the "coffee house"

at 10 A. M. to see the persons he wanted to get
in touch with (during the coffee break); one
morning he had breakfast there at 9 o'clock. But
his journal contains no reference to coffee houses
in Williamsburg.

(In Clark, Travels, I, #80, John is confused
with his father, Jacques, a Huguenot refugee after
the revocation of the Edict of Nantes who settled
in England. John and several of his brothers came
to America.)

86. Ford, Timothy

Travel diary, October 1785-November 1786, in South
Carolina Historical and Genealogical Magazine,
XIII (1912), 132-147, 181-204.

Ford traveled from New Jersey to Charlestown
by boat, without stopping in Virginia.

87. Fothergill, John (1676-1744)

An Account of the Life and Travels in the Work of
the Ministry, of John Fothergill....London: Luke
Hinde, 1753. 372 p.

A typical Quaker missionary journal, recording impressions of the effectiveness of meetings.
But congregations are not specifically located
geographically, and nothing is said about the non-
spiritual lives of the members. Fothergill made
three trips to America (in 1706, 1721 and 1736)
and visited Virginia Quakers on each journey.

Clark, Travels, I, #81

88. Franklin, James

The Philosophical & Political History of the
Thirteen United States of America....London:
J. Hinton & W. Adams, 1784. 156 p.

    A compilation from other sources, notably
Burnaby. Franklin pronounced Virginia women good
housewives, dancing when they were not sewing.
Pages 92-93 describe Williamsburg, whose buildings were "indifferent"; but, like Burnaby, he
concluded, "Upon the whole, Williamsburg is by
no means a disagreeable residence."

Clark, Travels, I, #241

89. [French Engineers]

"Journal of the Siege of York in Virginia (Engineers),"
Magazine of American History, IV (1880), 449-452.

    Brief, day-by-day account of the Yorktown
siege operations. Precise detail on engineer-
ing operations and the action of batteries.

90. Frost, Amariah

Staples, Hamilton B., ed., "A Diary at Mount
Vernon," American Antiquarian Society Proceedings,
1st ser., 1879, pp. 71-79.

    The entire journal covers a trip from Milford,
Mass., to northern Virginia, with stops at all the
principal cities along the way; the published part
is the entry for June 26, 1797, describing a visit
to Mount Vernon: the estate, hosts, other guests,
dinner and conversation.

91.   Gano, Rev. John (1727-1804)

Biographical Memoirs...Written Principally by
Himself. 151 p. New York: Southwick &
Hardcastle, 1806. Printed in part as "A Chaplain
of the Revolution...," Historical Magazine, V
(1861), 330-335.

       A Baptist minister from New Jersey, Gano
preached to congregations in the lower Shenandoah
Valley and in Frederick County and made two missionary itinerations into the Carolinas. During
the Revolution, he served under Sullivan in New
York and as chaplain in Clinton's brigade when
the army moved into Virginia. He did not arrive
in Yorktown until after the surrender, and his
brief reminiscences about the campaign, written
in his old age, do not include comments on Tidewater Virginia.

Clark, Travels, I, #242

92.   Garrettson, Freeborn (1752-1827)

The Experience and Travels of Mr. Freeborn Garrettson,
Minister of the Methodist Episcopal Church in North-
America....Philadelphia: Printed by Joseph Crukshank,
1791. 252 p.

       Garrettson itinerated in Virginia in 1777-78
and 1781-82. He preached against war but supported
the movement for local church autonomy expressed by
the Methodist conference at Manakin Town. His travel
journal therefore reveals something of the position
of a conscientious objector in revolutionary Virginia
as well as conditions within the Methodist organization.

Clark, Travels, I, #243

93.   Gilpin, Thomas, ed.

"Journal and Transactions of the Exiles, Citizens of Philadelphia, Sent to Winchester, Virginia, from 2d September, 1777, to 30 April, 1778," in Exiles in Virginia: with Observations on the Conduct of the Society of Friends during the Revolutionary War....(Philadelphia: C. Sherman, 1848), pp. 65-233.

The papers of the twenty Quaker exiles are concerned largely with efforts to secure their release from confinement in Winchester and arrange for their return to Philadelphia; this is not a travel journal, and there are no references to Tidewater Virginia.

Clark, Travels, I, #247

94.   [Gordon, Lord Adam (c. 1726-1801)]

"Journal of an Officer in the West Indies Who Travelled over a Part of the West Indies, and of North America, in the Course of 1764 and 1765," in Newton D. Mereness, ed., Travels in the American Colonies (New York: Macmillan, 1916), pp. 369-453.

Colonel Gordon was stationed in the West Indies with his Regiment of Foot, the 66th. He spent four months in the islands and then traveled on the continent from Florida to Canada. After a month in Virginia in the spring of 1765, he concluded: "Upon the whole, was [it] the case to live in America, this Province, in point of Company and Climate, would be my choice in preference to any, I have seen." In addition to the people and the natural resources, he described the towns of Williamsburg, Norfolk, Yorktown and Gloucester.

95.   [Gordon, Harry]

Account of the Battle of the Monongahela River...
from an Original Document of One of the Survivors.
Ed. by Francis Orpen Morris. London: Groombridge
& Sons, 1854. 10 p.

     The "Survivor" has been identified as Harry
Gordon, an artillery engineer serving with Colonel
Thomas Dunbar's Regiment. The journal records
the long march from Alexandria to Ft. Cumberland,
Indian negotiations and military preparations before the battle, Braddock's march and defeat and
death.

Clark, Travels, I, #250

96.   Gordon, James (1713-1768)

"Journal of Col. James Gordon, of Lancaster
County, Va.," William and Mary Quarterly, 1st ser.,
XI (1902-1903), 98-112, 195-205, 217-236; XII,
1-12.

     This Scotch-Irish Presbyterian came to
Virginia in 1738 and settled in the Northern
Neck as a planter-merchant. His journal con-
sists of brief daily entries about farming,
business and family affairs, his own health,
local events and amusements. There are references to members of the family and business
agents on visits to Williamsburg but no account
of their activities in the capital city. The
journal is valuable for details about life on
a plantation more nearly "average" than Westover
or Nomini Hall; there is the same hospitality,
for example, but Colonel Gordon expresses an
attitude that must have been fairly common when
he writes: "Our company still with us, with the
addition of Mr. Wormley, his wife & daughter, which
is rather troublesome at this time." (The guests
interfered with pressing business affairs.)

97. Gottschalk, Matthias Gottlieb. See MORAVIAN
MISSIONARIES

98. Graham, Samuel (1756-1831)

Memoir of General Graham, with Notices of the
Campaigns in Which He was Engaged from 1779 to
1801. Ed. by his son, Col. James J. Graham.
Edinburgh: Privately printed, 1862. 318 p.,
portrait, plates, maps. Printed in part anon.
as "A Recollection of the American Revolutionary
War," Virginia Historical Register, VI (1853),
204-211.

       Memoirs with a biographical sketch. Graham,
serving with Cornwallis as a captain in the 76th
Highlanders, came to Virginia in March 1781. He
describes activity in the York-James peninsula,
first with Arnold and Phillips, then with
Cornwallis: a surprise attack by William and
Mary students on the outskirts of Williamsburg,
the battle of Green Spring, the siege of Yorktown,
the surrender and march to prison camp at
Winchester.

Clark, Travels, I, #251

99. Gregory, William

"William Gregory's Journal, from Fredericksburg,
Va., to Philadelphia, 30th of September, 1765,
to 16th of October, 1765," William and Mary
Quarterly, 1st ser., XIII (1904-1905), 224-229.

       If William Gregory, Scot merchant in
Fredericksburg, regularly kept a diary, it has
not survived; we have only the account of this
trip, which briefly describes travel conditions

and accommodations but is largely devoted to
impressions of the Pennsylvania city. He mentioned conversations about the Stamp Act and
concluded: "The people here [in Philadelphia]
don't talk half so much of the stamps as they
do in Maryland and Virginia."

100. Griffith, John (1713-1776)

A Journal of the Life, Travels, and Labours in
the Work of the Ministry of John Griffith.
London: James Phillips, 1779. 427 p. Also
printed in Friends' Library, V (1837).

    A Welsh Quaker who settled near Philadelphia
in 1726, Griffith made frequent missionary journeys into the surrounding country and in 1765
came into the Valley of Virginia. His comments
are confined to religious conditions in the lives
of the Quakers whom he visited.

Clark, Travels, I, #88

101. Gronovius, Johannes Fredericus (1690-1760)

Flora Virginica, Exhibens Plantas Quas...
Johannes Clayton in Virginia Observavit atque
Collegit....Lugduni Batavorum [Leyden, Holland]:
apud Cornelium Haak, 1739-1743. 2 vols. in 1.

    John Clayton came to Virginia in 1705
and settled on the Piankatank River at Winsor,
where he planted and tended a botanical garden
of Virginia specimens collected in travels
throughout the middle Tidewater area--north
to the Rappahannock, south to the James, and
west to the Blue Ridge. He corresponded with
leading European and American botanists and
sent them seeds and specimens; Gronovius

classified the specimens, with the collabora-
tion of Linnaeus, and published the list under
the title Flora Virginica. The book, therefore,
is not a travel account though it represents
half-a-century of travel. Clayton's scientific
achievements were formally recognized in Virginia
when he was made the first president of the
Society for the Promotion of Useful Knowledge.

Clark, Travels, I, #89

102. Grove, William Hugh

MS Diary, 1698-1732, Travels in Great Britain
and the Netherlands and in America. Alderman
Library.

    Nothing is known of the author beyond the
fact that he was widely traveled. Of the American part of his journal (about 30 pp.) 23 pages
are devoted to Virginia, which he visited about
1731-1732. His description of Yorktown includes
ordinary rates and accommodations; in Williamsburg he was more interested in public buildings,
especially the College. He visited a number of
Tidewater plantations and described their architecture, crops, farming methods, slaves, living
accommodations and food. Though Grove's journal
often reminds the reader of Hugh Jones' Present
State, his impressions of Virginia seem to be
his own.

103. Hadfield, Joseph

An Englishman in America, 1785: Being the Diary
of Joseph Hadfield. Ed. by Douglas S. Robertson.
Toronto: Hunter-Rose Co., 1933. 232 p.

Young Hadfield, in America collecting debts
due his father's mercantile firm, traveled in
Virginia with Robert Hunter. His American diary,
unlike Hunter's, did not include his Virginia experiences, which were summarized later from memory; they consist of such generalized statements
as to be of little value to the historian. Though
he claimed to have been "an inmate of some of the
houses of the leading characters of the country,
the Beverleys, Randolphs, Washington, Lees, etc.,"
there is no internal evidence of the association
and his attitude towards Virginians was unfavorable; he considered them violently anti-British.

104. [Hager, Rev. Heinrich]

Warhaffte Nachricht von Einer Hochteutschen
Evangelischen Colonie zu Germantown in nord-
Virginien in America, und derselben dringendliches
ansuchen an ihre Glaubens-genossen in Europe. 1720.
8 p. Reprinted in Henry S. Dotterer, ed., Historical Notes relating to the Pennsylvania Reformed
Church, I (1899).

A promotion pamphlet for church and school in
the Orange County Germantown settled in 1714.

Clark, Travels, I, #91

105. [Hall, F.]

The Importance of the British Plantations in
America to This Kingdom; with the State of Their
Trade, and Methods for Improving It; as also a
Description of the Several Colonies There.
London: Printed for J. Peele, 1731. 114 p.

A promotional tract dedicated to Sir Robert Walpole, valuable for the discussion of the balance of trade within the Empire. The author had lived and traded in America for "many years" and visited Virginia at some time before 1731; his "description" is an analysis of its natural resources, products and trade.

Clark, Travels, I, #92

106. "The Halsey-Ramsey Diary. Unique and Original Insight Into Events During the Years 1779-1782," Pathfinder Mag., Nos. 36-39 (September 8, 15, 22, 29, 1894).

The joint diary of two officers of the Continental army in charge of a remount depot.

107. Hamilton, Henry (d. 1796)

Journal in John D. Barnhart, ed., Henry Hamilton and George Rogers Clark in the American Revolution. Crawfordsville, Indiana: R. E. Banta, 1951. 244 p.

"Report by Lieutenant-Governor Henry Hamilton on His Proceedings from Nov., 1776, to June, 1781," Historical Manuscripts Commission, Report on the Manuscripts of Mrs. Stopford-Sackville, of Dayton House, Northamptonshire (Herford, England, 1910), II, 223-248. Also printed in Michigan Pioneer and Historical Collections, IX (1886), 489-516.

After his capture at Vincennes by George Rogers Clark, Governor Hamilton was sent to prison in Williamsburg. His journal and report contain the best description we have of the Public Gaol, and his comments on the persons with whom he came in contact are especially valuable because his viewpoint was unusual. The journal ends with the entry of June 16, 1779, the day he arrived in Williamsburg, but the report covers the whole period of his residence here.

Clark, Travels, II, #35, 36

108. Handrup, Vitus. See MORAVIAN MISSIONARIES.

109. Hanger, George, Baron Coleraine (1751?-1824)

The Life, Adventures, and Opinions of Col. George
Hanger. London: Debrett, 1801. 2 vols.

As a captain in the Yager Corps, Hanger was on
active duty in the Carolinas until the fall of 1780,
when he contracted yellow fever and went to Bermuda
for his health. He therefore missed the Yorktown
campaign and was never in Virginia.

Clark, Travels, I, #214

110. Harrower, John (d. 1777)

The Journal of John Harrower, An Indentured Servant
in the Colony of Virginia, 1773-1776. Ed. with an
introd. by Edward Miles Riley. Williamsburg: Colonial Williamsburg, Inc., 1963. 202 p., illus.,
maps. Published in part American Historical Review,
VI (1900-1901), 65-107. MS Colonial Williamsburg.

During a depression in the Shetland Islands,
Harrower left home in search of employment. Unable
to find passage to Holland, he went to London instead
and looked in vain for clerical work. Finally, on
January 26: "This day I being reduced to the last
shilling I hade was oblidged to engage to go to
Virginia for four years as a schoolmaster for Bedd,
Board, washing and five pound during the whole time."
His ship arrived in Hampton Roads at the end of April
and docked at Fredericksburg on May 10, and indentures
were sold. Skilled craftsmen left the ship first;
Harrower did not find a master until May 26, when
Col. William Daingerfield of Belvidera bought his
indenture. When the diary volume ended two years
later, the Scotsman was still living happily and
gratefully with the Daingerfield family.

Harrower's diary is similar to Fithian's but
contains more information about his own clothing and

accommodations and more about indentured servitude.
Belvidera was a smaller plantation than Nomini Hall
and its style of living and entertaining less extravagant. Harrower's education was not so good as
Fithian's, but he was more mature and more interested
in the other employees; the love story of Lucy the
housekeeper and Anthony the overseer, for example,
is a superb commentary on human nature in any age.

111. Hartwell, Henry, James Blair and Edward Chilton

The Present State of Virginia, and the College. Ed.
with an introd. by Hunter Dickinson Farish. Williamsburg: Colonial Williamsburg, Inc., 1940. 105 p.,
plates, facsims., portraits.

        The analysis was written in 1697 but not pub-
lished until 1727. The authors were officials in the
government and the college--Councillor, President of
the College of William and Mary, and Attorney General,
respectively. Though the emphasis is political, the
book contains data about Virginia society, education
and religion.

Clark, Travels, I, #97.

112. Hazard, Ebenezer (1745-1817)

MS Journal of Journeys to the South, 1777-78. 2 vols.
(Virginia portion, 1777: May 22-July 3, Nov. 11-Dec. 17.)
Historical Society of Pennsylvania, MS No. 1398. Photo-
stat Colonial Williamsburg. Printed in part in Virginia
Magazine of History and Biography, LXII (1954), 400-423.

        Hazard was a New York bookseller who came South
twice in 1777 as Surveyor-General for the Post Office.
He made notes on each trip, probably for the American
geography which he never wrote; his friend, Jedidiah
Morse, however, did use them. Hazard was an experienced traveler, a discriminating and understanding
critic. He recorded not only geographical and economic data about the Virginia country-side and all
the towns he visited (Alexandria, Dumfries, Frederricks-
burg, Williamsburg, Jamestown, Suffolk) but also the

unusual machines and institutions that caught
his attention, travel conditions, and impressions
of people. His description of mid-war Williamsburg is the most complete I have seen. While in
town, from May 31 to June 10; he heard Bracken
preach at Bruton, with Governor Henry in the congregation; he attended a benefit ball for Peter
Pelham at the Capitol; he presented a memorial to
the House of Delegates suggesting that post masters
and post riders be exempted from military duties.

113. Heath, Major General William

Memoirs of Major-General Heath. Containing Anecdotes, Details of Skirmishes, Battles, and other
Military Events, during the American War. Written
by Himself. Boston: I. Thomas and E. T. Andrews,
1798. 388 p.

Heath was left in command of the American army
on the Hudson during the Yorktown campaign. Full
daily journal entries describe the campaign as
viewed from the northern army.

114. Hite, Major Isaac

"Memo. copied from the note-book of Maj. Isaac Hite,
Jr., of 'Belle Grove,' Frederick County, Va.,"
William and Mary Quarterly, 1st ser., X (1901),
121-122.

Brief diary of the siege of Yorktown, written
by an aide to General Muhlenberg. Military only.

115. Holme, Benjamin

A Collection of the Epistles and Works of Benjamin
Holme. To which is Prefix'd, an Account of His Life
and Travels in the Works of the Ministry...Written
by Himself. London: Luke Hinde, 1753. 194 p.

Holme, a Quaker minister in Yorkshire, spent
about five years in America "scattering the truth
and confounding the priests." He visited individual Quakers and held meetings in the Norfolk area
during the fall of 1715 but paid little attention
to the non-spiritual phases of the lives of the
people he met.

Clark, Travels, I, #101

116. Honeyman, Robert (1747-1824)

Colonial Panorama, 1775: Dr. Robert Honeyman's
Journal for March and April. Ed. by Philip
Padelford. San Marino: Huntington Library, 1939.
86 p., maps.

MS Diary, January 2, 1776-March 11, 1782. Library
of Congress. Film Colonial Williamsburg.

After brief service in the British navy as a
surgeon, Dr. Honeyman came to America and settled
in the Scotch Presbyterian area of Hanover County,
Virginia, as a planter-physician. In the spring of
1775 he paid a visit to relatives in Newport and
kept a journal of the trip, which led Mr. Padelford
to call him the "perfect eighteenth-century tourist."
Though he was not an ardent patriot, he joined the
Hanover militia and marched to Williamsburg, where
he performed medical services; he was present at
the siege of Yorktown. His MS diary is a little
history of the Revolution in Virginia--all phases
of it. After the war he enjoyed success in his
profession, a prominent place in Virginia society
and leisure to indulge his literary tastes. His
eldest son inherited his practice, the largest
share of his estate, and the most cherished family heirloom, "a human rib...which is of James
the fifth King of Scotland."

Clark, Travels, I, #257

117. Hoskens, Jane Fenn

The Life and Spiritual Sufferings of that Faithful
Servant of Christ, Jane Hoskens, a Public Preacher
among the People Called Quakers. Philadelphia:
William Evitt, 1771. 16 p. Reprinted in Friends'
Library, I (1837), 440-473.

    The author came from London to Philadelphia as
an indentured servant. Her journeys into Virginia
in 1726 and 1744 were entirely missionary in interest,
and her journal records little of the people and
places visited.

Clark, Travels, I, #102

118. Hull, Henry (1765-   )

"Memoirs of the Life and Religious Labours of Henry
Hull, a Minister of the Gospel, in the Society of
Friends, Late of Stanford, in the State of New York,"
Friends' Library, IV (1840), 233-304.

    Most of Hull's missionary work was done in
Pennsylvania, New York and New England, but he
made a trip south in 1799. At Leesburg he held a
meeting in the courthouse with two Methodist min-
isters. He then traveled up the Valley to New
Market, crossed Rockfish Gap, stopped at Lynchburg
(where he held a public meeting in the Mason's Hall),
and went on into Kentucky. Like many other Quakers,
he preached against slavery and the slave trade. He
was concerned about the condition of the slaves but
also had much to say about the influence of the system on the children of slave-holders, teaching them
pride and ungoverned passions. Unlike most critics,
he tried to do what he could for individual slaves:
preaching to them, of course, and leaving tips and
"good meat on the plate" for those who served him
at table. (See pp. 260-261 for a statement of his
views.)

119. Hunter, Robert, Jr. (1764-1843)

Quebec to Carolina in 1785-1786. Being the Travel
Diary and Observations of Robert Hunter, Jr., a
Young Merchant of London. Ed. by Louis B. Wright
and Marion Tinling. San Marino: Huntington Library,
1943. 393 p., maps.

   When the elder Hunter sent an agent to America
to settle his firm's overdue accounts, the son went
along for the business experience. He had already
received a gentleman's education and made the grand
tour of Europe; and, equipped with letters of introduction to prominent citizens of Canada and the
United States, he was prepared to make the trip an
adventure. He established Virginia headquarters at
the home of a cousin Archibald McCall, Scot merchant
at Tappahannock. Since young Hunter was more interested in sight-seeing and frolicking than in business
affairs, his journal's chief value is to the social
historian. In obedience to his father's request that
he keep a diary (to train him in accurate observation
and methodical reports), he made daily entries that
present sincere and enthusiastic impressions of
Virginia society; however lacking in literary merit
it may be, it is interesting because Hunter was a
good observer and reporter of things that interested
him.

Clark, Travels, II, #98

120. Hussey, Robert. See MORAVIAN MISSIONARIES.

121. Hutchins, Thomas (1730-1789)

A Topographical Description of Virginia, Pennsylvania,
Maryland, and North Carolina, comprehending the Rivers
Ohio, Kenhawa, Sioto, Cherokee, Wabash, Illinois,
Mississippi,...London: Printed for the Author, 1778.
67 p., 2 maps.

As a military engineer Hutchins traveled extensively in the western parts of the states described. No Tidewater Virginia data.

Clark, Travels, I, #258

122. Janson, Charles William

The Stranger in America: Containing Observations Made during a Long Residence in that Country, on the Genius, Manners and Customs of the People of the United States; with Biographical Particulars of Public Characters; Hints and Facts Relative to the Arts, Sciences, Commerce, Agriculture, Manufactures, Emigration, and the Slave Trade.... London: Printed for James Cundee, 1807. 499 p.

Janson lived in America from 1793 until about 1805; he was in Norfolk in 1800-1801 and in the Virginia backcountry in 1804. His attitude toward American people and institutions was hypercritical because he failed in business and found people unsympathetic and uncongenial. His observations, often freely borrowed from Morse, Weld and others, seem to have been his own in his descriptions of the town of Norfolk and a riot and yellow fever epidemic there in about 1801.

Clark, Travels, II, #99

123. Jarratt, Devereux (1733-1801)

The Life of the Reverênd Devereux Jarratt, Rector of Bath Parish, Dinwiddie County, Virginia. Written by Himself, in a Series of Letters Addressed to the Rev. John Coleman....Baltimore: Warner & Hanna, 1806. 223 p.

Autobiographical letters written in old age, the first one dated 1794. The "journal" is of special value for the early history of Methodism in Virginia. Though he was a minister in the Church

of England, he had been converted under Presbyterian influences and always preached a "vital"
religion, as distinguished from the Anglican for-
malism of his day.

The account of his early life in the first
letter is useful for a vivid picture of the ordinary lives of ordinary people in upper Tidewater
Virginia in the middle of the eighteenth century.

124. Jefferson, Thomas (1743-1826)

Notes on the State of Virginia. Ed. with an introd.
and notes by William Peden. Chapel Hill: Published
for the Institute of Early American History and
Culture by the Univ. of North Carolina Press, 1955.
315 p., map.

Though Jefferson's Notes is usually regarded
as an organized statement of his personal interests
and philosophy, it is also the classic description
of post-war Virginia, written by the person who, of
all his contemporaries, understood the state best.

For personal details of his life in Williamsburg, see his autobiography and letters. The ten-
volume edition of his writings, ed. by Paul L. Ford,
1892, is the most reliable; the twenty-volume edition, Lipscomb and Bergh, 1903, is more comprehen-
sive; the Princeton edition of his Papers, ed. by
Julian Boyd and others, will supercede all earlier
editions.

Clark, Travels, I, #262

125. Jones, Hugh (c. 1692-1760)

The Present State of Virginia. Ed. with an Introduction by Richard L. Morton. Chapel Hill: Published for the Virginia Historical Society by the
Univ. of North Carolina Press, 1956. 295 p.

After five years in Virginia--first as rector
of the Jamestown Church, then as professor of mathematics at the College of William and Mary--Hugh
Jones went back to England and wrote this book
about the colony "for the use of all persons concerned in the Virginia trade and plantation." The
first edition appeared in 1724; Mr. Morton's new
edition is especially useful because of its introductory sketch of Jones and the Virginia he knew
and for its full notes and index. Jones was an
accurate observer, interested in "more than bare
philosophy and speculative ethicks," and wrote with
the precision of a mathematician; his book, therefore,
is a reliable and compact guide to Virginia in the
first quarter of the eighteenth century and easily
the best picture of Williamsburg and its institutions,
its people and their way of life.

Clark, _Travels_, I, #107

126. Keith, George (1639?-1716)

A Journal of Travels from New-Hampshire to Caratuck,
on the Continent of North America....London: Joseph
Downing for Brab. Aylmer, 1706. 92 p.

Keith, once a Quaker, came to America as a
missionary for the Society for the Propagation of
the Gospel in Foreign Parts, to counteract the work
of Quakers in the colonies. When he preached in
Virginia in the spring of 1703, his congregations
were Anglicans, and he made no mention of Quakers
here, as in the other colonies. He arrived at
Yorktown in a sloop from Newcastle, then came on
to Williamsburg, where Governor Nicholson received
him and his party and Commissary Blair entertained
them kindly and hospitably at his home. He preached
at Yorktown, Williamsburg, Kikotan (where he heard
Blair preach also, and where his hostess was Blair's
daughter, a Quaker-turned-Anglican). In Gloucester
he preached at Abingdon Church and lodged at
Major Burwell's. He returned to Maryland via
Yorktown.

The Journal contains little of his travels or experiences outside the churches where he preached; it is more a record of sermons and denominational disputes than a travel account.

Clark, Travels, I, #108

127. Keith, Sir William (1680-1749)

A History of the British Plantations in America... Part I. Containing the History of Virginia; with Remarks on the Trade and Commerce of that Colony. London: Printed at the expense of the Society for the Encouragement of Learning, 1738. 187 p., map. (No other volumes published.)

While Keith was surveyor-general of customs for the southern colonies (1714-1716), just before he became governor of Pennsylvania, he made a tour through Virginia and presumably gathered the information used later in England when he wrote the History. The body of the volume is a history of the seventeenth century, with the last few pages sketches of Nicholson and Spotswood as public officials and builders of Williamsburg; his judgment of Spotswood, of course, is colored by his own association with him. His remarks on trade and government, pp. 177-187, express his mercantilistic criticism of imperial policy and present suggestions for improving Virginia's place in the system.

128. [Kimber, Edward (1719-1769)]

Itinerant Observations in America. Savannah: J. H. Estill, Printer, 1878. 64 p. Reprinted from the London Magazine, 1745-1746. Also in William and Mary Quarterly, 1st ser., XV (1907), 143-159, 215-224; and Georgia Historical Society Collections, IV (1878), 3-64.

The anonymous author has been identified as Edward Kimber, son of the Rev. Isaac Kimber, editor of the London Magazine, 1732-1755. (See notes on

the Kimbers in Sidney A. Kimber, "Relation of a Late
Expedition to St. Augustine," Papers of the Bibliographical Society of America, XXVIII (1934), Part II.)
Young Kimber visited Virginia early in December 1742
and made notes for a book of travels he planned to
write later; the article in his father's magazine
seems to have been all that he did with the project.
His "observations" are largely reminiscences dressed
up with classical allusions and rhapsodic passages
on the beauties of nature. When he crossed the
Chesapeake, for example, he saw satyrs as well as
dolphins and porpoises and envisioned Diana behind
every wave and shrub. He had only enthusiastic
praise for the generosity and occasional opulence
of Virginia hospitality on the Eastern Shore and
again in the Lower Peninsula. Beneath his literary
conceits the historian can find useful data about
agricultural products, trade between the eastern
and western shores, the physical appearance of Williamsburg, Yorktown and Norfolk, roads and travel
conditions. His impressions of the people and customs in Virginia are confused with those in Maryland
and too general to be of much value.

129. Kirkwood, Capt. Robert (1756-1791)

The Journal and Order Book of Captain Robert Kirkwood
of the Delaware Regiment of the Continental Line, ed.
by Joseph B. Turner. (Papers of the Historical Society of Delaware, LVI). Wilmington: Historical Society
of Delaware, 1910. 277 p.

    Kirkwood's "Journal of the Marches of the
Delaware Regiment of the Continental Line in the
Southern Campaign 1780-1782," pp. 9-30, records the
movements of his troops in the Carolinas. They
passed through Virginia in May 1780, sailing from
Head of Elk to Petersburg and marching South from
there; on the return trip in March 1782 they followed the same route, with brief stops in the
Piankatank and Rappahannock rivers. No comments
on the Virginia scene.

An Irish non-commissioned officer in the Ninth
Regiment of Foot, Lamb was captured at Saratoga, escaped and joined the Royal Welch Fuzileers. After
service in the Carolinas, he became a prisoner of
war at Yorktown, escaped, was re-captured at Fredericksburg, escaped again, was again re-captured, fled
to Philadelphia, and escaped through New Jersey and
New York. His journal includes a brief description
of the siege of Yorktown, but the most valuable part
of his account deals with his experiences as a prisoner of war.

Clark, Travels, I, #268

133. La Rochefoucauld-Liancourt, Francois Alexandre
     Frédéric, Duc de (1747-1827)

     Travels through the United States of North America,
     the Country of the Iroquois, and Upper Canada, in
     the Years 1795, 1796, and 1797; with an Authentic
     Account of Lower Canada. London: R. Phillips, 1799.
     2 vols.

     The Duke came to Norfolk from Charleston in
May 1796 and visited Hampton, Yorktown and Williamsburg; then he went through Richmond, Petersburg,
Monticello, Staunton and Winchester to Maryland.
Since he was a political economist, his observations
center around the state's government and politics,
taxation, finances, trade (with tables of exports
from Norfolk and comments on trade with Philadelphia),
current prices, farming methods and natural resources.
He also described the cities and towns visited, commented on travel conditions and hospitality, and in
his summary, "General Observations on Virginia," included his impressions of the people. Much of his
information came from John Marshall, Thomas Jefferson,
and Bishop Madison (his guide to Williamsburg; hence
his emphasis on the college in his description of the
town).

     This translation leaves much to be desired in
accuracy and style; the first edition (Paris, 1799),
therefore, should be consulted when exact wording is
wanted.

Clark, Travels, II, #103

130. Krafft, J. C. P. von

"Journal of Lieutenant J. C. P. von Krafft, 1778-
1784," New York Historical Society Collections, XV
(1882), 1-202.

Krafft served with Hessian regiments in the
British army 1778-1783. His journal covers service
in the North during the later years of the Revolution, principally in the garrison of New York.
There is good information on the situation there
during the period of the Yorktown campaign.

131. Lafayette, Marie Joseph Paul Yves Roch Gilbert de
Motier, Marquis de (1757-1834)

The Memoirs, Correspondence and Manuscripts of
Marquis de Lafayette. London: Saunders & Otley,
1837. 3 vols.

This is the English edition of Mémoires,...
et Manuscrits du Général Lafayette, publiés par sa
Famille (Paris, 1837-48, 6 vols.) and includes the
reminiscences of his "Second Voyage to America, and
Campaigns of 1780 and 1781" and "Historical Memoirs
of 1779, 1780, and 1781." The narrative is sketchy
and wholly military; it is written in the third person and includes actions in which he did not partic-
ipate.

Clark, Travels, I, #267

132. Lamb, Roger (1756-1830)

An Original and Authentic Journal of Occurrences
during the Late American War....By R. Lamb, late
Serjeant in the Royal Welch Fuzileers....Dublin:
Wilkinson & Courtney, 1809. 438 p. Another ver-
sion of the journal appeared as the Memoir of His
Own Life by R. Lamb. Dublin: J. Jones, 1809.
296 p.

135. Lauzun, Armand Louis de Gontaut, Duc de (1747-1793)

Memoirs of the Duc de Lauzun. Tr. by C. K. Scott-
Moncrieff. New York: G. Routledge & Sons, 1928.
253 p.

Lauzun and his legion served in Gloucester during the siege of Yorktown, which he described in a
brief, factual account colored by his dislike for the
American troops, especially the Virginia militia commanded by Weedon. This part of his Memoirs has been
printed separately in Magazine of American History, VI
(1881), 51-53, and in American Historical Magazine, II
(1907), 292-298.

Clark, Travels, I, #200 (as Duc de Biron)

136. Lee, Henry (1756-1818)

Memoirs of the War in the Southern Department of the
United States. New edition with revisions and a bi-
ography of the author by Robert E. Lee. New York:
University Publishing Co., 1870. 620 p.; illus. in-
clude surrender of Cornwallis and plan of Yorktown
Siege.

A detailed account of the southern campaigns
by a participant who wrote with the confident judgment of a competent military leader. "Light Horse
Harry" Lee had been serving with Greene in the
Carolinas but was on detached duty in Virginia at
the time of the Yorktown siege and took part in
the operation. The Memoirs contain an excellent
account of the surrender ceremony.

Clark, Travels, I, #269.

137. Lee, Lucinda

Journal of a Young Lady of Virginia, 1782. Ed. by
Emily V. Mason. Baltimore: John Murphy and Co.,
1871. 56 p.

134. Latrobe, Benjamin Henry (1764-1820)

The Journal of Latrobe, Being the Notes and Sketches
of an Architect, Naturalist and Traveler in the United
States from 1796 to 1820. With an introd. by J. H. B.
Latrobe. New York: D. Appleton and Co., 1905. 269 p.
Illus. include: sketches of Edmund Randolph, George
Washington, Patrick Henry, Travels on Horseback in
Virginia; views of Billiards at a Country Tavern,
James River Falls, Norfolk from Town Point, Mount
Vernon, Richmond.

Latrobe landed at Norfolk in March 1796 and
spent the next two years in Virginia, with headquarters first at Norfolk, then at Richmond. He was already recognized in England as an able architect and
engineer, and letters of introduction to prominent
persons in Virginia assured him of a warm reception
here. He was consulted by private citizens about re-
modeling their houses and by corporations and State
officials on improvements in the Dismal Swamp and
navigation of the James and Appomattox rivers. In
Richmond he designed the penitentiary building and
finished the Capitol. He went to Philadelphia in
March of 1798 and later worked in Washington, D. C.,
in Kentucky and in New Orleans.

This volume contains selections from the journals rather than the complete text. The artist's
manuscripts, sketchbooks and single drawings are
scattered among several individuals and institutions;
probably all those relating to his Virginia visit be-
long to Mrs. Ferdinand C. Latrobe of Baltimore. Many
scholars have used the manuscript journals and quoted
from them, notably Talbot Hamlin in Benjamin Henry
Latrobe (New York: Oxford Univ. Press, 1955). Thomas
T. Waterman and John A. Barrows, Domestic Colonial
Architecture of Tidewater Virginia (Chapel Hill: Univ.
of North Carolina Press, 1947) contains a transcrip-
tion of the diary entry relating to Green Spring, and
a negative of the watercolor sketch of the mansion is
owned by the Virginia 350th Anniversary Commission.

A series of letters to a friend describing a
series of visits to Lees, Washingtons, and other
families in the Northern Neck. Lucinda's interest
in dancing, flirting, playing cards and pranks was
probably typical of teen-age girls of the larger-
planter class, and her descriptions of amusements,
food, fashions, and personalities are lively and
entertaining.

Clark, Travels, II, #111

138. Lewis, Charles

"Journal of Captain Charles Lewis, October 10-
December 10, 1755," Virginia Historical Society
Collections, n.s., XI (1891), 203-218.

Col. Charles Lewis of Caroline, son of John
Lewis of Warner Hall, went to Ft. Cumberland under
Major Andrew Lewis of Augusta County. His journal
is made up of daily entries which mention travel
conditions, roads, food, clothing, condition of
the men and the land they passed through. His description of the fort is unusually good.

139. Macaulay, Alexander (1754-1798)

Journal, February 1783, in William and Mary Quarterly,
1st ser., XI (1902-1903), 183-191.

This young Scotsman came to Virginia during the
Revolutionary years, married Elizabeth Jerdone, and
established a mercantile business in Yorktown. For
the amusement of a friend, he recorded a trip from
Jerdone Hall, Louisa County, to Yorktown. His style
is mannered and his humor heavy-handed, but the
account includes good detail about roads and accommodations at inns along the way. His sardonic description of Williamsburg, though puerile, is re-
deemed by the all-too-rare appearance of landladies
on the scene--Mrs. Campbell, her daughter Molly, and
Mrs. Craig.

140. McClellan, Joseph

"Diary of the Pennsylvania Line, May 26, 1781–April 25, 1782," <u>Pennsylvania State Archives</u>, 2nd ser., XI: <u>Pennsylvania in the War of the Revolution, Battalions and Line, 1775-1783</u> (1880), 677-727.

Captain McClellan's journal ends June 13, 1781, when he left the field. The remainder of the "Diary" is Lieutenant Feltman's journal, listed above as No. 81. McClellan's record adds new detail about the movements of the Pennsylvania brigade in Virginia during the early summer of 1781.

141. McDowell, William

"Journal of Lieut. William McDowell, of the First Penn'a Regiment, in the Southern Campaign, 1781-1782," <u>Pennsylvania Archives</u>, 2nd ser., XV (1893), 295-340.

McDowell served with Wayne's Pennsylvania brigade in the Virginia campaign. His journal covers the period May 26, 1781–December 21, 1782.

142. Mackenzie, Frederick

<u>Diary of Frederick Mackenzie, giving a Daily Narrative of His Military Service as an Officer of the Regiment of Royal Welch Fusiliers during the Years 1775-1781 in Massachusetts, Rhode Island and New York</u>. Cambridge: Harvard University Press, 1930. 2 vols.

An informative journal of the campaigns of the Revolution as seen from British headquarters in America. Mackenzie was in New York in 1781 as deputy adjutant-general to Clinton.

143. MacPherson, Donald

Letter from Donald MacPherson, a Young Lad Who Was
Sent to Virginia with Captain Toline, in the Year
1715....London, 1720. Broadside. Also in R.
Jamieson, ed., Letters from a Gentleman in the North
of Scotland to His Friend in London (London, 1822),
I, 206-209.

    The young Scot became an indentured servant in
Maryland, rather than Virginia. The letter to his
father, dated June 2, 1717, describes his work at
Portobago--largely watering horses and serving at
table. His master had come to America as an indentured servant and was now a well-to-do planter who
lived "almost as well as the Lairt o'Collottin."

Clark, Travels, I, #118

144. M'Robert, Patrick

A Tour through Part of the North Provinces of America: Being, a Series of Letters Wrote on the Spot,
in the Years 1774, & 1775. Edinburgh: Printed for
the Author, 1776. 47 p. (Offprint from the
Pennsylvania Magazine of History and Biography,
April, 1935, ed. by Carl Bridenbaugh.

    One of the best travel accounts, by a well
educated and discerning Scot. But he did not come
to Virginia.

145. Makemie, Rev. Francis (1658-1708)

A Plain and Friendly Perswasive to the Inhabitants
of Virginia and Maryland for Promoting Towns and
and Cohabitation. By a Well-wisher to Both Govern-
ments. London: J. Humfreys, 1705. 16 p. Also in
Virginia Magazine of History and Biography, IV (1897),
255-271.

Makemie was a Presbyterian "preacher, a doctor
of physic, a merchant, an attorney, a counsellor at
law, and, which is worse of all, a disturber of gov-
ernments," first in Maryland and then for many years
on the Eastern Shore of Virginia. While the purpose
of his pamphlet was to state the advantages of towns,
he included in his argument glowing descriptions of
Virginia's climate, soil, natural resources and advantages for promoting trade.

Clark, Travels, I, #119

146. Martin, Joseph Plumb (1760-1850)

Private Yankee Doodle, Being a Narrative of Some of
the Adventures, Dangers and Sufferings of a Revolutionary Soldier. Ed. by George F. Scheer. Boston:
Little, Brown and Co., 1962. 301 p. Printed anon.
in 1830 as A Narrative...

In seven years of Service with Connecticut
infantry units and then with the Corps of Sappers
and Miners, Martin rose from private to sergeant.
He wrote his Narrative long after the events he
described, but his remarkable memory--supplemented
no doubt by a diary of some sort and perhaps by
other narratives--supplies colorful details of all
phases of a soldier's daily life. The narrative is
bright with pleasant moments, humor, and original
glimpses of high ranking officers as well as other
privates. He passed through Williamsburg going
from Burwell's Ferry to Yorktown but did not describe the town.

147. Maussion, Gaston de

They Knew the Washingtons; Letters from a French
Soldier with Lafayette and from His Family in
Virginia, tr. by Princess Radziwill. Indianapolis:
Bobbs-Merrill Co., 1926. 255 p.

The editor states that Gaston de Maussion came
to Virginia in 1781 and fought at Yorktown with

Lafayette's army. Two letters written from Williamsburg November 4 and 5 describe military conditions in the peninsula. After the war he brought his family to Virginia and settled on a plantation near Mount Vernon, where he was overseer. His comments and those of his wife on plantation life in Virginia in the late 1780's and 1790's include colorful glimpses of Washington and Mrs. Washington at Mount Vernon, but their authenticity is doubtful.

Clark, _Travels_, I, #291

148. Mazzei, Philip (1730-1816)

Memoirs of the Life and Peregrinations of the Florentine, Philip Mazzei, 1730-1816. Tr. by Howard R. Marraro. New York: Columbia Univ. Press, 1942. 447 p. Printed in part in _William and Mary Quarterly_, 2nd ser., IX (1929), 161-174, 247-264; X (1930), 1-18.

Mazzei, a Florentine physician and wine merchant, came to Virginia in the fall of 1773. Since he planned to introduce grape culture, he brought along several Italian workmen to plant and tend his vineyards. His ship put into Hampton Roads and he made his way to Williamsburg, stopping off at "the home of Mr. Eppes," whom he identified as Jefferson's brother-in-law. This was Francis Eppes of Eppington, who was probably visiting at the Wayles family seat, the Forest. There and in Williamsburg he met the merchant Thomas Adams (his "mentor"), Washington, Wythe and others who were in town for the meeting of the General Assembly. When he left James City County, he planned to settle in the Valley but stopped at Monticello, where he lived as Jefferson's guest until his own dwelling house at Colle was completed. There he planted his vineyards and experimented with other crops.

His _Memoirs_, written long after the Revolution, emphasize his part in the war and in the fight for religious liberty in Virginia.

Clark, _Travels_, I, #273

149. Meacham, Rev. James (1763-1820)

"A Journal and Travel of James Meacham," Trinity
College Historical Society Papers, IX (1912),
66-95; X (1913), 87-102.

Meacham was a native of Sussex County. After
the Revolution he became an itinerant Methodist minister, serving the Williamsburg Circuit in 1791.
For that year his journal contains entries only
from July to December. He was present in Williamsburg on July 14, when he heard Brother O'Kelly preach
in the Capitol.

After 1792 he preached in Mecklenburg, Portsmouth and North Carolina. His journal contains good
material on early Methodism but is entirely concerned
with religious matters except in his special interest
in slavery, the subject of sermons and private ad-
monitions to members of his congregations.

150. Michel, Francis Louis

William J. Hinke, ed. and tr., "Report of the Journey
of Francis Louis Michel from Berne, Switzerland, to
Virginia, October 2, 1701-December 1, 1702," Virginia
Magazine of History and Biography, XXIV (1916), 1-43,
113-141, 275-288. Illus. include: Map of Entrance to
Chesapeake Bay, sketches of College of William and
Mary, Bruton Church, the Capitol, 3 Indians and their
Houses.

After brief service as an officer in the French
Army, Michel came to Virginia planning to organize
a Swiss settlement. Though he did not found a colony,
his reports led to the organization of a joint-stock
company, George Ritter and Company, under whose aus-
pices Christopher von Graffenried founded New Bern,
North Carolina.

Michel's report to prospective settlers included
almost everything they would need to know about Virginia:
geography and climate of the Tidewater area, the land
system and arrangements for tenants, opportunities for

artisans to find work, travel and living conditions, food and houses. He included also a detailed account of the voyage to Virginia--accommodations, prices, and ship-board etiquette. He visited and described Williamsburg, Yorktown, Gloucester, and the Huguenot settlement at Manakintown. He was in Williamsburg in May 1702, when he attended and described the ceremonies attending the death of William III and proclamation of Queen Anne.

151. Mitchell, John (d. 1768)

The Present State of Great Britain and North America, with Regard to Agriculture, Population, Trade, and Manufactures....London: Printed for T. Becket and P. A. de Hondt, 1767. 363 p., map.

Dr. Mitchell, graduate of the University of Edinburgh, was a cartographer and botanist as well as a physician. He practiced medicine in Virginia for twenty-five years, first in Middlesex County, then at Urbanna.

The most valuable part of the book is the famous Mitchell map. The text is largely arguments with respect to the economic policy of the Empire. Dr. Mitchell maintained that the tobacco colonies were potentially the most useful area in the Empire for developing effective mercantilism but that the over-emphasis on tobacco had worn out the lands; he recommended opening up new lands in the West and producing other agricultural staples.

Clark, Travels, I, #124

152. Montrésor, Capt. John (1736-1799)

The Montrésor Journals..., ed. by G. D. Scull. New York: New-York Historical Society, 1882. 578 p.

The volume includes the journal of Col. James Montrésor, 1757-1759, as well as that of his son Capt. John Montrésor, 1757-1778.

The younger Montrésor was wounded in the Braddock campaign, then served as chief of engineers with Howe in Boston. His journal concerns Virginia only in Howe's 1777 expedition from New York to Philadelphia via the Chesapeake and Head of Elk. Military only.

Clark, Travels, I, #278

153. Mooers, Benjamin

"Major-General Benjamin Mooers, of Plattsburg, N. Y.," Historical Magazine, 3rd ser., I, (1872), 92-94.

Short autobiography written in old age, with brief reminiscences of the siege of Yorktown. Mooers was lieutenant and adjutant in Hazen's Canadian Regiment.

154. MORAVIAN MISSIONARIES

Rev. William J. Hinke and Charles E. Kemper, eds., "Moravian Diaries of Travels through Virginia," Virginia Magazine of History and Biography, XI-XII (1903-1905).

Manuscripts from the archives of the Moravian Church at Bethlehem, Pennsylvania, translated by Hinke and edited by Hinke and Kemper. After 1743, itinerant Moravian missionaries visited Virginia repeatedly, following this route: Bethlehem, Lebanon, Lancaster, York, Frederick, Hagerstown, and across the Potomac and down the Shenandoah Valley by the Great Waggon Road of the Fry-Jefferson Map. Their journals are more informative than those of Quakers or Methodists, for they mention natural features, travel conditions, and names of Germans visited, and they describe living conditions as well as spiritual ones. None of them visited Tidewater Virginia, however. Extracts printed here include:

"Diary of Leonhard Schnell and John Brandmueller
of their Journey to Virginia, October 12-December 12,
1749," XI, 115-131; XII, 81-82.

"Report and Observations of Brother Gottschalk on his
Journey through Virginia and Maryland,Undertaken in
March and April, 1748," XI, 225-234.

"Diary of Journey of Brothers Joseph [August Gottlieb
Spangenberg] and Matthew Reutz through Maryland and
Virginia in July and August, 1748," XI, 235-242.

"Diary of Leonhard Schnell and Robert Hussey, of
their Journey to Georgia, November 6, 1743-April 10,
1744," XI, 370-393.

"Diary of Journey of Rev. L. Schnell and V. Handrup
to Maryland and Virginia, May 29-August 4, 1747,"
XII, 55-61.

"Diary of Brother Gottschalk's Journey through
Maryland and Virginia, March 5-April 20, 1748,"
XII, 62-80.

"Diary of the Journey of the First Colony of Single
Brethren to North Carolina, October 8-November 17,
1753," XII, 134-153, 271-281.

155. Moré, Charles Albert, Chevalier de Pontgibaud,
     Comte de (1758-1837)

     A French Volunteer of the War of Independence...Tr.
     and ed. by Robert B. Douglas. New York: D. Appleton
     and Company, 1898. 294 p.

     Moré, a soldier of fortune, wrote his memoirs
in later life and his memory was not entirely accurate.
His account of the Revolution includes his arrival in
the Chesapeake on board a French ship, a brief visit
to Williamsburg, where Governor Jefferson gave him a
pass to the American army at Valley Forge, and brief
reminiscences of the Yorktown campaign.

Clark, Travels, I, #279

156. Moreau de Saint-Méry, Médéric (1750-1819)

Moreau de St. Méry's American Journey [1793-1798].
Tr. and ed. by Kenneth Roberts and Anna M. Roberts....
Introd. by Stewart L. Mims. Garden City: Doubleday
and Co., 1947. 394 p.

    A refugee from the Jacobin régime, Moreau de
St. Méry landed at Norfolk in March 1794 and remained for two months with other French refugees in
the Norfolk-Portsmouth area. His description of
their life is sprightly and entertaining--he wrote
it with some care later--but reliable enough because
he made diary entries on the spot. His chief interest was people: pretty women (with charming voices
but big feet), public amusements (the theatre, a May
Day celebration, cockfighting), Negroes on Sundays
and holidays, weddings, funerals. But he included,
too, comments on trade with Philadelphia and Baltimore, the local market and prices, rail fences,
communications and military fortifications. In a
later section devoted to Philadelphia he added bits
of information about Virginia, notably in essays on
slavery and indentured servitude.

Clark, Travels, II, #108

157. Morse, Jedidiah (1761-1826)

The American Universal Geography, or, a View of the
Present State of all the Empires, Kingdoms, States,
and Republics in the Known World, and of the United
States of America in Particular. Boston: Isaiah Thomas
and Ebenezer T. Andrews, 1793. 2 vols. Maps.

    Morse's Geography is more interesting than other
gazetteers because he had traveled extensively along
the Atlantic seaboard and was interested in social
customs and manners as well as economics and politics.
His description of Virginia is full of contrasts and
contradictions. His personal impressions, derived
from a stay of about a month, were almost entirely
unfavorable because Virginians were not congenial to
his Federalist politics or his strict Calvinist

standards of religious and social behavior. On the
other hand, he acknowledged "free" use of Jefferson's
Notes. His dismal picture of Williamsburg's post-war
society was immediately challenged in A Letter from
St. George Tucker, Esq., Professor of Law in the
College of William and Mary, to The Reverend Jedediah
Morse, Author of The American Universal Geography
(first printed in Richmond, 1795, by Thomas Nicolson;
reprinted in William and Mary Quarterly, 1st ser., II
(1903-1904), 181-203; original letter, in Library of
the College of William and Mary, reprinted Richmond,
1953, by the William Byrd Press for the Institute of
Early American History and Culture).

Clark, Travels, II, #109

158. Morton, Thomas

"Morton's Diary," Virginia Historical Register, IV
(1851), 143-147.

    Morton kept an ordinary in New Kent; this is his
day book, and the fragmentary diary is on its front
leaves. It is concerned with the unsuccessful expedition against the Shawnees, led by Major Andrew
Lewis in the spring of 1756. (See George Washington's
letter to Dinwiddie, Winchester, April 7, 1756, in
Fitzpatrick, Writings, I, 300-304.)

159. Munson, Dr. Eneas

"Siege of Yorktown, 1781," in Benson J. Lossing,
Hours with Living Men and Women of the Revolution.
New York, 1889.

    Dr. Munson was a surgeon's mate in the Connecticut
Line, apparently serving with the Light Infantry at
Yorktown. This account was related to Lossing and
transcribed by him in 1848.

160. Murray-Pultenay, Sir James (1751-1811)

Letters from America 1773 to 1780; being the Letters
of a Scots officer, Sir James Murray, to his Home during the War of American Independence. New York: Barnes
& Noble [1950]. 90 p.

    Sir James came to America in 1776 and served in
the unsuccessful siege of Charleston, then in New
York, New Jersey and Pennsylvania. After 1777 he
was stationed in the West Indies and therefore did
not take part in the Yorktown campaign.

Clark, Travels, I, #280

161. Muse, Col. Hudson

Letter to Thomas Muse, Northumberland Courthouse,
April 19, 1771, in William and Mary Quarterly, 1st
ser., II (1903-1904), 239-241.

    Colonel Muse described a trip to Williamsburg,
where he "spent the time very agreeably, at the plays
every night."

162. Nourse, James

"Journey to Kentucky in 1775: Diary of James Nourse,
Describing his Trip from Virginia to Kentucky...,"
Journal of American History, XIX (1925), 121-138,
251-260, 351-364.

    Nourse was a London woolen draper who came to
Virginia with his family in 1769, arriving at
Hampton May 10. He lived there a year, then moved
to a plantation near Charleston, West Virginia.

    This diary contains no data about his early
experiences in Virginia and no mention of the Tidewater.
His itinerary was from his plantation to Pittsburgh,
then down the Ohio by flatboat and on to Harrodsburg
and Boonesboro on foot.

163. Ogden, Aaron

"Autobiography of Col. Aaron Ogden, of Elizabeth-
town," New Jersey Historical Society Proceedings,
2nd ser., XII (1892-1893), 13-31.

Reminiscences of the Revolution. Ogden served
at Yorktown with the New Jersey brigade, but there
is very little reference to the siege.

164. Oldmixon, John (1673-1742)

The British Empire in America, Containing the
History of the Discovery, Settlement, Progress and
State of the British Colonies on the Continent and
Islands of America. 2nd edition, London, 1741.
2 vols.

A compilation, rather than a travel account,
which leans heavily on Beverley and Hugh Jones.
The descriptions of Williamsburg (I, 406-409) and
Virginia people (I, 427-429), however, are useful.

165. Orme, Robert (d. 1781)

"Captain Orme's Journal," in Winthrop Sargent,
The History of an Expedition against Fort Du Quesne.
...(Philadelphia: Lippincott, Grambo & Co., 1855),
pp. 281-359.

Orme entered the army as an ensign in the 35th
Foot and later exchanged into the Coldstream Guards,
of which he became a lieutenant. (He was never pro-
moted to the rank of captain.) He probably obtained
a leave of absence in order to accompany Braddock,
with whom he was a great favorite. "As bold in the
boudoir as on the battle-field" he made a favorable
impression wherever he went.

His journal opens with his arrival at Hampton
February 20, 1755, whence General Braddock set out
immediately for Williamsburg to meet Commodore Keppel

and arrange the disposition of the troops. Orme
records Braddock's conversations with Dinwiddie
and the decision to use Alexandria as headquarters.
The group accordingly left Williamsburg March 22,
accompanied by Dinwiddie. The account deals wholly
with the problems of supply and other military
matters and contains nothing of personalities or
local conditions.

        For an analysis of Sargent's book, see Clark,
Travels, I, #233, 250, 306.

166. Owen, Nicholas (d. 1759)

A View of Some Remarkable Axcedents in the Life of
Nics. Owen on the Coast of Africa and America from
the Year 1746 to the Year 1757" in Eveline Martin,
ed., Journal of a Slave-Dealer (Boston: Houghton
Mifflin, 1930). 120 p. Illus. from Owen's sketches.

        Owen was a resident slave trader in Sierra Leone
who made six trips to America, selling slaves in the
West Indies, Rhode Island and Philadelphia. Although
he did not come to Virginia, his autobiography contains useful information about the slave trade in
most of its phases, and the editor's introduction is
especially intelligent.

167. Palmer, Esther (d. 1714)

Journals of 3 missionary journeys, 1704-1705, in
Journal of the Friends' Historical Society, VI
(London, 1909), 38-40, 63-71, 133-139.

        This Quaker woman, a native of Long Island, did
extensive missionary work in the American colonies
and in England. In the three journeys recorded here
she traveled more than 3,000 miles on horseback; her
itineraries are summarized below:

First journey, late in 1704, "The Journal of Susanna
Freeborn and Esther Palmer from Rhoad Island to and in
Pennsylvania, &c." They did not come into Virginia on
this trip.

Second journey, spring and summer of 1705, "The
Journal of Esther Palmer & Mary Lawson, from
Philadelphia to Maryland, Virginia, and Carolina
& from thence back to Philadelphia again." Journal entries are brief but give their itinerary
and names of hosts, with comments on accommodations,
places of meeting and sometimes the attendance. The
women visited Quakers in the Northern Neck, Charles
City County, Jamestown and Nansemond County. About
their stay in the Peninsula they wrote: "We went to
Ann Acres 30 Miles & by ye Way Call'd at ye Gover-
nours at Williams Burrough (at his request) who
treated us Kindly. On ye 4th day [of the week,
late in April] we had a Meeting at ye Widw Acres;
on ye 6th day we went to Kickatan to meeting 28
Miles from the Widdows." (See Thomas Story's
fuller account of this visit.)

Third trip, end of summer, 1705, "A Jornall off
Mary Banister and Esther Palmers Travells In
Maryland and Virginei," about two weeks in Accomac
and Northampton counties.

The journals as a whole are useful for a study
of Virginia Quakers, for they identify them and furnish approximate locations of their homes.

168. Parkinson, Richard (1748-1815)

A Tour in America in 1798, 1799, and 1800. Exhibit-
ing Sketches of Society and Manners, and a Partic-
ular Account of the American System of Agriculture,
with its Recent Improvements. London: Printed for
J. Harding, 1805. 2 vols. First published as The
Experienced Farmer's Tour in America....London:
John Stockdale, 1805. 735 p. Extracts appeared as
George Washington; Statement of Richard Parkinson.
Baltimore: Lord Baltimore Press, 1909. 38 p.

The author came to America to rent one of
Washington's farms, but the land was poor and he
settled down instead near Baltimore. The book is
a treatise on agriculture rather than a travel
account; however, it "abounds in curious details"
about Washington.

Clark, Travels, II, #113

169. Pemberton, John

"The Life and Travels of John Pemberton, a Minister of the Gospel of Christ," Friends' Library, VI (1842), 267-380.

    This Philadelphia Quaker did most of his missionary work in Europe. He came to Virginia during the Revolution as one of the group of Pennsylvania Quakers sequestered in the Shenandoah Valley. Pages 287-300 of this article contain entries from his diary which describe the imprisonment; his more famous brother Israel, merchant-philanthropist, was a member of the same group of exiles.

170. Pickering, Timothy (1745-1829)

Selections from his journal and letters in Octavius Pickering, The Life of Timothy Pickering (Boston: Little Brown, 1867, 4 vols.), I, 297-299.

    As adjutant general of the Continental Army, Pickering was in Virginia from September to November, 1781. His Journal contains brief comments on Alexandria, Mount Vernon, Dumfries, Fredericksburg, Williamsburg, and the Tidewater countryside between Alexandria and Williamsburg. His descriptions of Botetourt's statue and coach are among the best we have.

171. Popp, Stephen (1755-1820)

A Hessian Soldier in the American Revolution: The Diary of Stephen Popp. Tr. by Reinhart J. Pope. N.P.: Privately printed, 1953. 39 p., maps and charts.

    Translation, by a descendant of Stephen Popp, of the manuscript diary in the library of the Bayreuth Historical Society. The diary, beginning in Bayreuth in January 1777 and ending there in

December 1783, was probably put together later from
brief notes made at the time of the events recorded.
Popp was in Virginia from May 1781 through January
1782--at first with his regiment, then as a prisoner
of war in Winchester--and his account of experiences
there includes comments on the country, climate,
crops, travel conditions, and attitudes of Virginia
people as well as colorful descriptive notes on camp
life.

After the Revolution, Popp returned to Bayreuth,
where he spent the rest of his life as a musician.

Clark, Travels, I, #288

172. Potter, Cuthbert

A Journal and Narrative of a Journey made by me
Cuthbert Potter from Middx. County in Virginia to
Boston in New England in Newton D. Mereness, ed.,
Travels in the American Colonies (New York: Macmillan,
1916), pp. 4-11.

Potter made this trip in the late summer of
1690 as agent of Governor Nicholson, delivering
official letters and investigating political conditions along the route. The journal opens with
his departure from Ralph Wormeley's house and
records the itinerary via the head of Chesapeake
Bay, Newcastle, Philadelphia, New York, Newport,
Boston and return. There are no comments on conditions in Virginia.

173. Quincy, Josiah (1744-1775)

"A Journal, 1773," in Josiah Quincy, III, Memoir
of the Life of Josiah Quincy Jun. of Massachusetts
(Boston: Cummings, Hilliard & Co., 1825), pp. 73-141.
Complete text in Massachusetts Historical Society
Proceedings, XLIX (1915-1916), 424-481.

While still in his twenties, young Quincy became one of Boston's leading lawyers and patriots.
With John Adams he defended Capt. Thomas Preston
in the Boston Massacre trial while his loyalist
brother Samuel acted for the Crown. Toward the end
of 1772 he developed symptoms of pulmonary tubercu-
losis and on the advice of his physician made the
trip South for his health. He went to Charleston
by sea and returned to Boston overland, with a ten-
day stop in Virginia early in April. He was an intelligent but critical observer of Southern people
and institutions, especially slavery.

In Virginia he visited and described Suffolk,
Smithfield, and Williamsburg. Though he found
Virginia farmers less literate than those in Massachusetts, he was favorably impressed with their farms
and agricultural methods. He pronounced Williamsburg
"inferior to my expectations. Nothing of the population of the north, or of the splendour and magnif-
icence of the south." His own interest in politics
led him to the Capitol, of course; the General
Assembly was not in session, but he attended a
hearing in the General Court and spent an evening in
"wholly political" conversation with two members of
the Council. From this evidence he concluded that
the Virginia court system was "amazingly defective,
inconvenient, and dangerous, not to say absurd and
mischievous." The Council Chamber, however, was
"furnished with a large, well chosen, valuable
collection of books, chiefly of law."

Clark, Travels, I, #290

174. R., J.

The Port Folio: or A View of the Manners and Customs
of Various Countries: Interspersed with Anecdotes of
Former Times. In Letters to a Friend. By J. R.,
Late Captain in the Royal Lancashire Militia, and
formerly of the Royal Fuzileers. London: Dean and
Schultze, 1812. 2 vols.

In this series of letters written in 1811 and
1812, "J. R." reminisces about his youthful travels

all over the world, and his observations extend
all the way from the philosophical and practical
ideas of Hindoo women and Portugese peasants to his
own notions of the best way to organize and dis-
cipline an army. In America as an officer in the
British Light Infantry, he claimed to be "a partic-
ipater in most of the scenes described." The Virginia
portion of his reminiscences is contained in three
letters in Volume II, pp. 91-116. The letter of
January 27, 1812 describes military action on the
James River with emphasis on the Westover and Petersburg areas and Mrs. Byrd and Mrs. Bolling, Virginia
hostesses to the British troops. The letter of
January 29 relates the story of the heroism of
Mrs. Bolling's most distinguished ancestor, Pocahontas
--a garbled account--and comments on the Virginia
proclivity for gambling. The January 31 letter describes the siege of Yorktown and attempts to relieve
Cornwallis of responsibility for its outcome, then
outlines briefly the march of prisoners to Frederick,
Maryland, with comments on travel conditions and the
prevalence of "military inn keepers" along the way.

Clark, _Travels_, I, #261

175. Revel, Gabriel Joachim du Perron, Comte de (1756-1814)

Journal Particulier d'une Campagne aux Indes
Occidentales (1781-1782). Paris: H. Charles-
Lavauzelle, [1898?]. 287 p. Illus. include map
of Gloucester and of Yorktown and environs.

     Du Perron came to America with the fleet under
de Grasse in March 1781 and participated in the siege
of Yorktown as an infantryman. His journal describes
conditions in Gloucester--the morale of the French
troops, the English hospital there, his impressions
of the American soldiers and civilians.

Clark, _Travels_, I, #293

176. Revel, James

The Poor Unhappy Transported Felon's Sorrowful
Account of His fourteen Years Transportation at
Virginia in America. In Six Parts. London, Printed
and Sold in Stonecutter-Street, Fleet-Market, [1750?].
8 p. Poem.

The subtitle summarizes the narrative: "Shewing,
How his Father having only this one Son, made him his
Darling, and when he was old enough put him Apprentice
to a Tin-man, near Moorfields, where he got into bad
Company. How he ran away from his Master, and went
a robbing with a Gang of Thieves. How his Master got
him back again, but he would not be kept from his
wicked Companions, but went thieving with them again.
How he was transported for fourteen Years. With an
account of the way the Transports work, and the
Punishment they receive for committing any Fault.
Concluding with a word of advice to all young Men."

Revel worked in the tobacco fields of a master
whose plantation was on the upper waters of the
Rappahannock. Just before his indenture ended, his
master died and the unhappy felon went into the service of a Jamestown cooper, who arranged his return
to England.

Clark, Travels, I, #139 and 294

177. Reutz, Matthew. See MORAVIAN MISSIONARIES.

178. Richardson, John (1667-1753)

An Account of the Life of that Ancient Servant of
Jesus Christ, John Richardson...and His Services
in the Work of the Ministry, in England, Ireland,
America &c....London: Luke Hinde, 1757. 236 p. Also
printed in Friends' Library, IV (1840).

Richardson was an English Quaker whose missionary work in America was largely in Pennsylvania. In

Virginia, 1701 and 1732, he criticized roads and ferries, taxes, Presbyterians and Anglicans.

Clark, Travels, I, #141

179. Riedesel, Friederike Charlotte Luise von (1746-1808)

Letters and Memoirs relating to the War of American Independence....New York: G. & C. Carvill, 1827. 323 p.

Madame Riedesel followed her husband General Riedesel to America, where he was serving with Burgoyne. The Riedesels were captured at Saratoga and traveled with the other prisoners of war from Boston to Albemarle County, Virginia. After hardships of bad weather and roads, crude accommodations, and the hostility of Americans along the way, they found a warm welcome at Colle, Philip Mazzei's plantation near Monticello, and spent six pleasant months there. Her comments on life in Virginia are brief but direct.

Clark, Travels, I, #295

180. [Ritson, Mrs. Anne]

A Poetical Picture of America, Being Observations Made, during a Residence of Several Years, at Alexandria, and Norfolk, in Virginia; Illustrative of the Manners and Customs of the Inhabitants; And Interspersed with Anecdotes, Arising from a General Intercourse with Society in that Country, from the Year 1799 to 1807. By a Lady. London: Printed for the Author, 1809. 177 p.

The husband of this English lady established himself as an American merchant, first in Alexandria, then in Norfolk. She joined him in 1799. A bad poet but a good observer, her picture of Norfolk is full of unusual details of interest to the social and economic historian: housekeeping problems and methods; foods available at the city market (with prices and imports); dress; private amusements;

public occasions (weddings, funerals, church services,
holidays, the theatre, public "gardens", races); the
yellow fever epidemic; treatment of Negroes; ladies'
gardening; the absence of intellectual life because
Dunmore burned the town.

Clark, Travels, II, #118

181. Robertnier, Louis Jean Baptiste Silvestre de

MS Journal des guerre faites en Amérique pendans les
années, 1780, 1781, 1782, 1783 avec quelques disser-
tations sur les moeurs & coutumes des américains....
323 p. Rhode Island Historical Society. Typescript,
trans. by Prof. Edouard R. Massey. Microfilm copy,
Colonial Williamsburg.

    Robertnier was a lieutenant in the Soissonnais
Regiment of Rochambeau's army. He stopped in Wil-
liamsburg September 27, 1781, en route to Yorktown.
After the surrender of Cornwallis he went to West
Point, where he paused to write his impressions of
Virginia: the people, their gardens, their method
of curing pork; the towns of Williamsburg, Yorktown
and West Point; Virginia geography and weather.

182. Robertson, Archibald (c. 1745-1813)

Archibald Robertson, Lieutenant-General Royal Engineers, His Diaries and Sketches in America, 1762-1780.
New York: New York Public Library, 1930. 300 p.

    Did not come to Virginia.

Clark, Travels, I, #297

183. Robin, Claude C.

New Travels through North-America: in a Series of
Letters....Tr. from the Original of the Abbé Robin.
Boston: Printed by E. E.Powers and N. Willis, for
F. Battelle, 1784. 95 p.

The Abbé Robin, a chaplain in the French
army, landed in Boston in June 1781 and came
South via Connecticut, New York, the Jerseys,
Philadelphia and Baltimore. A philosopher and
patriotic Frenchman, he was not a precise observer; he was interested rather in the national
character and future prospects of Americans, the
activities and good behavior of their French allies
(who introduced them to brass bands and faro).
Letter X, written in Williamsburg September 30,
describes the appearance of the town and surrounding countryside. Letter XI, dated Yorktown November 6, contains a general account of the battle
and surrender, comments on British-American hatred,
and describes destruction in the town with details
about books piled in heaps among ruined buildings.

Clark, Travels, I, #298

184. Rochambeau, Donatien-Marie, Vicomte de (1755-1813)

Rochambeau Father and Son....New York: Henry Holt
and Co., 1936. 285 p. Illus. include camps at
Archer's Hope and Williamsburg.

     The journal of the Viscount, translated by
Lawrence Lee, pp. 190-270, describes the trip to
Head of Elk, thence to the James River and Williamsburg; the advance against Yorktown and personal reflections on the siege. In addition to
military observations, the younger Rochambeau includes a description of Virginia.

185. Rochambeau, Jean Baptiste Donatien de Vimeur, Comte
de (1725-1807)

Mémoires Militaires, Historiques et Politiques....
Paris: Fain, 1809. 2 vols.

     Rochambeau's account of the Yorktown campaign
was written years after the events and based on his
own memory, supplemented with information from other
sources. Selections from the Mémoires, dealing with
the Yorktown siege only, are:

Relation, ou Journal des Opérations du Corps Francais sous le Commandement du Comte de Rochambeau...depuis le 15 d'Aout. Philadelphia: William Hampton, n.d.

Memoirs of the Marshall Count de Rochambeau Relative to the War of Independence of the United States. Extracted and translated by M. W. E. Wright. Paris: At the French, English, and American Library, 1838. 114 p.

Clark, Travels, I, #299 and 300

186. Rogers, Robert (1731-1795)

A Concise Account of North America....London: Printed for the Author, 1765. 264 p.

Major Rogers, commander of Rogers' Rangers, wrote this account of the American colonies for an English audience. He used first-hand knowledge of the areas he had visited, with supplementary data collected from "the most authentic materials." His only known trip into the South was the expedition against the Cherokees in 1761. His description of Virginia, therefore, was compiled from gazetteers and other travel accounts.

Clark, Travels, I, #301

187. Rose, Rev. Robert (1705-1751)

MS Diary, 1747-1751. 108 p. Colonial Williamsburg.

See Guide to the Manuscript Collections of Colonial Williamsburg, #34.

188. Rostaing, Juste Antoine Henry Marie Germain, Marquis de

MS journal of the Marquis de Rostaing, in Archives l'Inst. Guerre, Paris.

Rostaing was colonel of the Gatinois Regiment of Rochambeau's army at Yorktown.

189. Saint-Exupéry, Georges Alexander Cesar de

Countess Anais de Saint-Exupéry, tr., "The War Diary of Georges Alexander Cesar de Saint-Exupéry, Lieutenant in the Regiment of Sarre-Infantry," Legion d'Honneur, II, No. 2 (Yorktown Number, October, 1931), 107-113.

A translation, in the third person, of the parts of the journal that refer to the movements of de Grasse and Rochambeau. Entries are brief but informative.

190. Salley, John Peter

Fairfax Harrison, ed., "A Brief Account of the Travels of John Peter Salley, a German Who Lives in the County of Augusta in Virginia," Virginia Magazine of History and Biography, XXX (1922), 211-222.

Salley (or Salling) came to Augusta County from Pennsylvania in 1740. This journal is his account of a trip to the West in 1742-1745. He went down the Mississippi into the Illinois country, where he was captured by the French and taken to New Orleans, a prisoner of Bienville. After two years he escaped and returned home through Indian country, without touching Tidewater Virginia.

191. Salmon, Thomas (1679-1767)

A New Geographical and Historical Grammar....London: Printed for W. Johnston, 1762. 8th ed. 640 p., maps.

Though Salmon prepared his gazetteer after traveling widely in the West Indies, he did not visit Virginia.

Clark, Travels, I, #303, 304, 305

192. Savery, William (1750-1804)

A Journal of the Life, Travels and Religious Labors
of William Savery...Compiled from His Original Mem-
oranda, by Jonathan Evans. London: C. Gilpin, 1844.
316 p.

       A typical Quaker missionary journal, with no
description of places and people visited. Savery
made several trips into Virginia, but only that of
May 1795 is included in his extant journals; at
that time he visited Quaker settlements from
Alexandria to Richmond.

Clark, Travels, II, #119

193. Scattergood, Thomas (1748-   )

Journal in Friends' Library, VIII (1844), 1-225.

       Diary of a New Jersey Quaker who came to
Virginia in 1778, 1779, 1780, and 1786. The
entries are short and concerned largely with
Scattergood's communion with his own heart. Ex-
ceptionally dull, even for this kind of journal,
and quite useless to historians.

194. Schnell, Leonhard. See MORAVIAN MISSIONARIES.

195. Schoepf, Johann David (1752-1800)

Travels in the Confederation [1783-1784] from the
German of Johann David Schoepf. Tr. and ed. by
Alfred J. Morrison. Philadelphia: William J.
Campbell, 1911. 2 vols.

       Dr. Schoepf came to America in 1779 as surgeon
to the Hessians in the British army. After the
Peace of Paris he traveled extensively in the middle
and southern states and recorded his observations in
one of the best travel accounts we have. He entered

Virginia in the fall of 1783 via Leesburg and
traveled to Richmond, then down the peninsula to
Williamsburg and across the James River through
Southside Virginia into North Carolina.

His account of America (our geography, economy, politics, living conditions and customs) is
as precise and scientific as he could make it. In
some areas he borrowed information from other writers
when he did not visit the region described; in Tidewater Virginia, however, the observations seem to be
his own. His details about travel conditions include roads and ferries, tavern accommodations as
compared with private entertainment (with a note on
tavern signs), geological formations and crops that
could be seen from the road. Among towns described
are: Leesburg, Fredericksburg, Hanover Courthouse,
Richmond, Manchester, Petersburg, Williamsburg,
Yorktown, Jamestown, Smithfield, and Suffolk. Other
subjects of brief essays include: Virginia husbandry
(on small plantations as well as large ones), exports, gardens, the servant problem, use of mules,
use of lightning rods, governmental procedures,
courthouses, social democracy, the influence of
the Revolution on religion and the press, and
finally the Virginian way of life.

Clark, Travels, II, #120

196. Scott, Job (1751-1793)

A Journal of the Life, Travels, and Gospel Labours
of that Faithful Servant and Minister of Christ,
Job Scott. New York and London: James Phillips &
Son, 1797. 354 p.

A Quaker missionary journal. Scott, a native
of Providence, Rhode Island, did missionary work in
the middle and southern states, Great Britain and
Ireland. He spent six weeks in Virginia in 1789,
traveling from Alexandria to Richmond to Norfolk,
into North Carolina and back through the Valley. He
held "a small meeting" in Williamsburg, "a town where
no friends live." In Norfolk people behaved very
"undevoutly" at meeting, running in and out, talking,
laughing and gazing about; Scott reproved them, then

left with a heavy heart, "finding little open door
of utterance because there was scarce any door of
entrance into their hearts...."

Clark, Travels, II, #121

197. Serle, Ambrose (1742-1812)

The American Journal of Ambrose Serle, Secretary to
Lord Howe, 1776-1778, ed. with an Introduction by
Edward H. Tatum, Jr. San Marino: The Huntington
Library, 1940. 369 p., maps.

     The journal records briefly, pp. 239-53,
Admiral Howe's expedition from New York to Philadelphia via the Virginia capes and Chesapeake Bay.

Clark, Travels, I, #309

198. Seymour, William

A Journal of the Southern Expedition, 1780-1783.
Wilmington: Historical Society of Delaware, 1896.
45 p.

     Seymour's regiment only passed through Virginia
enroute to the Carolinas and did not take part in
the Yorktown campaign.

Clark, Travels, I, #310

199. Shepard, Samuel

"A Tory Returns to Buckingham: Extracts from Samuel
Shepard's Diary," William and Mary Quarterly, 2nd
ser., XV (1935), 411-412.

     Shepard was a Virginia Tory who returned to
his Buckingham County estate in 1776 after six
years in England. The first diary entry printed
here records a stop at a Maysville tavern, where

a friend asked his opinion of possible reconcilia-
tion with England. He answered the question at
some length and was immediately arrested and jailed
for treason. The jailer treated him surprisingly
well, explaining: "You are most fortunate in not
having old man Pat Henry at the tavern, he would
have addressed the people and you would have been
treated badly."

200. Simcoe, John Graves (1752-1806)

A Journal of the Operations of the Queen's Rangers,
from the End of the Year 1777, to the Conclusion of
the late American War. Exeter: Printed for the
Author, [1787]. 184 p. Illus. include: Skirmish
at Richmond, Landing at Burrell's, Skirmish at
Petersburg, Action at Osburns, Action at Spencer's
Ordinary.

       Simcoe took command of the Queen's Rangers in
October 1777 and was ordered to Virginia in December 1780. After the siege of Yorktown he returned
to England and later served as lieutenant-governor
of Upper Canada and governor of Santo Domingo. His
account of the Virginia campaign is detailed and
factual, and his maps are especially attractive.
(See the Simcoe Maps and Papers, Colonial Williamsburg Archives, for unpublished sketches of the city
of Williamsburg, Richmond, roads around New Kent
Church, roads in Gloucester, and a watercolor of
Yorktown.)

Clark, Travels, I, #311

201. Smith, Daniel (1748-1818)

The Journal of Daniel Smith. Introd. and notes by
St. George L. Sioussat. Nashville: Tennessee Historical Society, 1915. 66 p.

       A routine surveyor's journal, concerned with
running the line between North Carolina and Virginia,
Tennessee and Kentucky in 1779-1780. Though Smith

was a student at the College of William and Mary,
his journal was begun after he had left Tidewater
Virginia.

Clark, _Travels_, I, #312

202. Smith, Hezekiah (1737-1805)

Chaplain Smith and the Baptists, or, Life, Journals,
Letters and Addresses of the Rev. Hezekiah Smith,
D.D., of Haverhill, Massachusetts, 1737-1805. Ed. by
Reuben A. Guild. Philadelphia: American Baptist
Publication Society, 1885. 429 p.

      Instead of editing Smith's journals and other
papers, Editor Guild wrote a biography illustrated
with selections from Smith's writings. Though Smith
knew George Washington personally, there is no
evidence in this book that he ever visited him at
Mount Vernon or came into Virginia for any other
purpose.

203. Smith, Jacob

"Diary of Jacob Smith--American Born," _Pennsylvania_
Magazine of History and Biography, LVI (1932),
260-264.

      Smith was a Loyalist, serving from 1777 to
1781 with the Queen's Rangers. His diary contains
a brief but interesting daily account of the siege
of Yorktown.

204. Smith, Samuel (1759-1854)

Memoirs of the Life of Samuel Smith. _Being an_
Extract from a Journal Written by Himself, from
_1776 to 1786._ Middleborough, Massachusetts, 1853.
24 p. Reprinted as "Memoirs of Samuel Smith, Soldier
of the Revolution, 1776-1786," _Crumbs for Antiquarians_,
I (1860), 7-31.

A sketchy and doubtful narrative by a Rhode Island soldier who was present at Yorktown.

205. Smith, William Loughton (1758-1812)

Albert Matthews, ed., "Journal of William Loughton Smith, 1790-1791," Massachusetts Historical Society Proceedings, LI (1917), 20-76. Also printed separately Cambridge: The University Press, 1917. 88 p.

After completing his education in England and Switzerland, Smith came home to Charleston, South Carolina, and entered public life. In 1788 he was elected to Congress, became a leading Federalist pamphleteer, then followed John Quincy Adams as minister to Portugal.

The printed portion of his diary is concerned with two short trips made between sessions of Congress: into New England in 1790 and from Philadelphia to South Carolina in the spring of 1791. He entered Virginia from Washington, D. C., and stopped at Alexandria, Mount Vernon, Gunston Hall, Fredericksburg, Richmond, Manchester and other places in the Southside. He described Mount Vernon with Federalist zeal, the new Capitol at Richmond with restrained enthusiasm. (The following year he was to attack Jefferson in a pamphlet war.) He found the people of Southside Virginia uncomfortably housed but "polite and kind" to strangers, somewhat shiftless, spending their time on tavern piazzas arguing the relative merits of race horses. Their pronunciation of there (thar), mare (mar), etc. fascinated him in a repulsive sort of way. In Prince Edward County he heard a great deal about "the celebrated Patrick Henry, who is now making a great deal of money by large fees of £50 or £100 for clearing horse thieves and murderers, which has lost him much of the great reputation he enjoyed in his neighborhood...."

Clark, Travels, II, #125

206. Smyth, John Ferdinand Dalziel (d. 1814)

A Tour in the United States of America....London:
G. Robinson, 1784. 2 vols.

   The record of the author's life is confused
and fragmentary. Even his name is doubtful. He
seems to have changed it to Stuart, on the grounds
of double descent from the Duke of Monmouth. He
studied medicine at Edinburgh and came to Williamsburg to practice in about 1770. He was an active
Loyalist in the Revolution in Virginia and Maryland;
after his return to England in 1783 he drew an
annual pension of £300 for service as a captain in
the Queen's Rifles and for property losses in America.

   His book was written after the events described
and without dates; it is therefore difficult to
check details and evaluate the author's dependability
But his descriptions of the Virginia countryside and
places in the Hampton Roads area and his essays on
Virginia people and customs record lasting general
impressions that reflect personal observation and
experience. In Williamsburg he dined at the Raleigh
Tavern and attended horse races on the "very excellent course" on the edge of town. He described
Virginia people by "degrees of rank"--first, gentlemen of the best families and fortunes; second, about
half the white population, less polished and respect-
able than the first but often as well-to-do; third,
lower class, fewer in number than in other states;
fourth, Negroes, two-thirds of the population.

Clark, Travels, II, #62

207. Spangenberg, August Gottlieb. See MORAVIAN MISSIONARIES.

208. Spencer, Rev. William

MS Diary, 1790. 2 vols. Colonial Williamsburg.

See Guide to the Manuscript Collections of Colonial
Williamsburg, No. 39.

209. Stanton, Daniel

A Journal of the Life, Travels, and Gospel Labours
of a Faithful Minister of Jesus Christ, Daniel
Stanton....Philadelphia: Joseph Crukshank, 1772.
184 p. Reprinted in Friends' Library, XII (1848).

     A monotonous missionary journal, of little
use to secular historians. Stanton was a Quaker
who came to America in 1735 and worked in New
England and Pennsylvania until 1760, when he came
South for the first time. In Virginia he traveled
down the Shenandoah Valley, en route to the
Carolinas.

Clark, Travels, I, #153

210. Stedman, Charles (1753-1812)

The History of the Origin, Progress, and Termina-
tion of the American War. London: Printed for the
Author, 1794. 2 vols.

     A Philadelphia lawyer educated at the College
of William and Mary, Stedman was a Loyalist and
served throughout the war as Cornwallis' commissary.
His account of the war is the standard presentation
of the British interpretation. Military only.

211. Stevens, James

Diary, 1786-1787, in Virginia Magazine of History
and Biography, XXIX (1921), 385-400.

     The author was a Scotsman who had lived in
Virginia for eighteen years when he returned to
Glasgow to procure mill stones, bolting cloths
and other stores for his flour mill and business
establishment in Halifax County. This is the
journal of that trip.

The first page of the manuscript is muti-
lated; the legible part opens with his embarka-
tion at Norfolk, May 1786, and closes with his
return to Virginia the following January. Some
of his descriptions of experiences in Scotland
are useful for comparison with similar conditions
in Virginia: several trials and one execution, a
"great fair," a funeral ceremony.

212. Story, Thomas (1662-1742)

A Journal of the Life of Thomas Story: Containing,
an Account of his Remarkable Convincement of, and
Embracing the Principles of Truth, As held by the
People called Quakers; And also, of his Travels
and Labours in the Service of the Gospel....New-
castle-upon-Tyne: Printed by Isaac Thompson & Co.,
1747. 768 p.

The most readable and informative of Quaker
missionary journals. Story left England in 1698,
entered Chesapeake Bay in December and landed at
the mouth of Queen's Creek. On this first visit
he held a round of meetings in homes of Quakers
in the peninsula, visited the Chickahominy Indians
and then traveled on into North Carolina. He was
again in Virginia in the spring of 1705, when he
came to Williamsburg and was treated "with various
Sorts of Wines and Fruits, and much Respect" by
Governor Nicholson. After a long conversation on
doctrinal matters, Nicholson introduced the group
of Quakers to Commissary Blair, who gave them a
tour of the College buildings. In the Chapel
their guide explained, "Here we sometimes preach
and pray, and sometimes we fiddle and dance; the
one to edify, and the other to divert us."
Nicholson finally sent them on their way laden
with "portable Fruits" and "kind Expressions."

Clark, Travels, I, #156

213. [Tallmadge, Samuel (1755-1825)]

"Diary," in Orderly Books of the Fourth New York Regiment, 1778-1780, the Second New York Regiment, 1780-1783....(Albany: Univ. of the State of New York, 1932), pp. 739-785.

     Tallmadge, adjutant of the Second New York Regiment, came to Virginia in September of 1781. His diary makes brief reference to the destruction in Yorktown and contains some account of the fighting. After the surrender he marched overland to Baltimore through Williamsburg, New Kent, Fredericksburg, and Alexandria. No descriptions of the country or the people of Virginia.

Clark, Travels, I, #316

214. Tarleton, Sir Banastre (1754-1833)

A History of the Campaigns of 1780 and 1781, in the Southern Provinces of North America. London: T. Cadell, 1787. 518 p., maps and plans, including Yorktown.

     Tarleton came to America with Cornwallis as a volunteer. His History is not a travel account, for the descriptive and critical comments inserted into the narrative only reflect his personal egotism. However, useful documents relating to the narrative are included among his notes at the end of each chapter.

Clark, Travels, I, #317

215. Thacher, James (1754-1844)

A Military Journal during the American Revolutionary War, from 1775 to 1783....Boston: Cottons & Barnard, 1827. 487 p.

When Dr.Thacher became surgeon to the First
Virginia State Regiment in the fall of 1778, he
met General and Mrs. Washington, whom he describes
on pages 149-150, 157-160. He came to Virginia in
September 1781 with a Massachusetts regiment, and
his account of the siege of Yorktown is detailed
and personal, with emphasis on medical problems.
There are brief descriptions of Williamsburg and
Yorktown.

Clark, Travels, I, #318

216. Tilden, John Bell

"Extracts from the Journal of Lieutenant John Bell
Tilden, Second Pennsylvania Line, 1781-1782,"
Pennsylvania Magazine of History and Biography,
XIX (1895), 51-63, 208-233.

Tilden served with Wayne's brigade in the
Virginia campaign. His diary begins August 1,
1781, and extends to December 31, 1782, with
full entries on the siege of Yorktown and brieter
ones on the other parts of the campaign.

217. Tilghman, Tench (1744-1786)

Memoir of Lieut. Col. Tench Tilghman, Secretary
and Aid to Washington....Albany: J. Munsell,
1876. 176 p.

Tilghman's diary of the siege of Yorktown,
pp. 103-107, is a brief record of military events
written as rough notes.

See also two manuscripts in the Library of
Congress: Diary and accounts relating to services
for the Indian Commission dated from July 28, 1775,
to December 5, 1775 (36 p.) and Diary and accounts
relating to operations at Yorktown dated from
September 22, 1781, to October 18, 1781 (20 p.).

Clark, Travels, I, #254

218. Toulmin, Harry (1767-1823)

The Western Country in 1793: Reports on Kentucky
and Virginia by Harry Toulmin. Ed. by Marion
Tinling and Godfrey Davies. San Marino: Huntington
Library, 1948. 141 p.

  This Unitarian minister came to Virginia to
spy out the land for his English parishioners and
report to them on the suitability of the western
country for settlement. His journal, therefore,
is a collection of precise data obtained from his
own observation and from discerning inquiries
directed to well-informed inhabitants of the areas
in which he was interested. In Tidewater Virginia
he visited Norfolk, Urbanna and Richmond and commented on: houses, gardens, fences, farming methods
and products, live stock, food, clothing, servants,
opportunities for employment, taverns, religious
practices, character of the people. Everywhere he
went he made careful notes of prevailing prices in
Virginia currency, with the equivalent pound-sterl-
ing value.

Clark, Travels, II, #127

219. Trabue, Daniel (1760-1840)

Colonial Men and Times, containing the Journal of
Colonel Daniel Trabue..., ed. by Lillie Du Puy
Harper. Philadelphia: Innes & Sons, 1916. 624 p.

  A former officer in the Virginia militia, Trabue
was a sutler in Lafayette's army at the siege of
Yorktown. His naive diary of the siege throws interesting sidelights on its events.

Clark, Travels, I, #320

220. Trumbull, Jonathan (1740-1809)

"Yorktown, Virginia, Aug. 12-Nov. 5, 1781," Massachusetts Historical Society Proceedings,XIV (1875-
1876), 331-338. Microfilm copy of MS journal at
Colonial Williamsburg.

Trumbull was a lieutenant-colonel in the
Connecticut Line and military secretary to
Washington during the Yorktown campaign. His
diary constitutes an interesting daily military
account of the campaign from American army headquarters and contains brief descriptions of the
military situation in Williamsburg and of a Custis
funeral.

221. Tucker, St. George (1752-1827)

MS Diaries in Tucker-Coleman Papers, Colonial
Williamsburg. See Guide to Mansucript Collections of Colonial Williamsburg, #44.

Tucker's diary of the siege of Yorktown was
printed in the William and Mary Quarterly, 3rd ser.,
V (1948), 375-395. Two others, unpublished, are
travel diaries, recording trips to Edenton, North
Carolina, and to New York.

222. Uring, Nathaniel

A History of the Voyages and Travels of Capt.
Nathaniel Uring....London: J. Peale, 1726. 384 p.

Uring was an English seaman who came to
Virginia from the West Indies in 1699 with a cargo
of rum, molasses and codfish. In Hampton Roads
his ship and its cargo burned. Penniless and ill,
he managed to live by working on a James River farm.
His account of his stay in Virginia (which apparently lated only a few months) is not specific
enough to be of much value.

Clark, Travels, I, #163

223. Vail, Christopher

Christopher Vail's Journal, 1775-1782. Force
Transcript, Manuscripts Division, Library of
Congress. 40 p.

A fascinating narrative of military and
privateer service and prison life throughout the
American Revolution. Vail was not at Yorktown,
but saw the sloop <u>Bonetta</u> arrive in New York
after Cornwallis's surrender.

224. Van Cortlandt, Colonel Philip (1749-1831)

"Autobiography of Philip Van Cortlandt, Brigadier-
General in the Continental Army," <u>Magazine of American History</u>, II (1878), 278-298.

Colonel Van Cortlandt of the Second New York
Regiment wrote a good personal account of the
Yorktown siege.

225. Villebresme, Chevalier de

"Souvenirs du Chevalier de Villebresme sur la
Guerre d'Amérique (1779-1781)," <u>Le Carnet de la
Sabretache</u>, IV (1896).

Contains a detailed description of the surrender of Cornwallis.

226. Walker, Thomas (1715-1794)

<u>Journal of an Exploration in the Spring of the
Year 1750</u>. Boston: Little, Brown and Co., 1888.
69 p.

Dr. Walker, a native of King and Queen County, was a physician, merchant, politician, explorer, and chief agent of the Loyal Land Company. This journal records the first exploratory trip through Cumberland Gap into the valley of the Holston River.

Clark, Travels, I, #169

227. Washington, George (1732-1799)

The Diaries of George Washington, 1748-1799. Ed. by John C. Fitzpatrick. Boston: Houghton Mifflin Co., 1925. 4 vols.

Selections in George Washington Colonial Traveller, 1732-1775. Ed. by John C. Fitzpatrick. Indianapolis: Bobbs, Merrill Co., 1927. 416 p.

Washington was the most widely-traveled American of his day. Until he became commander-in-chief of the American army, he was in and out of Williamsburg as follows: 1748 July, Yorktown; [1749 May?]; 1750 June, Yorktown; 1752 January; 1753 October; 1754 January, July, October; 1755 May, August, November; 1756 March-April, June, December; 1757 April-May; 1758 March, May, December; 1759 January, February-March, April-May, October-November; 1760 April, October-November; 1761 April, November; 1762 March, May, November; 1763 April-May, October; 1764 January, April-May, June-July, November-December; 1765 May; 1766 April-May, November-December; 1767 February, March-April, November; 1768 April-May, October-November; 1769 May, November-December; 1770 May-June; 1771 May, July, October-November; 1772 March-April, November; 1773 March, November; 1774 May-June, August.

He usually rode horseback on these trips, using a gig or coach only if Mrs. Washington or the Custis children accompanied him. From Mount Vernon to Fredericksburg he followed the old Potomac Path in good weather; when the swampy road was almost impassable, he crossed the Potomac near Alexandria at Posey's Ferry, rode down the Maryland shore of the

river and re-crossed into King George County at
Hoe's Ferry. From Fredericksburg he followed
the road by West Point marked on the 1755 ed. of
the Fry-Jefferson map (now called Washington's
Burgess Route).

In Williamsburg he attended to military
affairs in the French and Indian War, to public
affairs (he was a Burgess for sixteen years),
and to personal matters connected with land spec-
ulation and plantation business. At the same time
he entered into the social life of the town.

Washington's diary entries are brief and
business-like, with little description. But
when supplemented by his ledger entries, they
reveal a great deal about tavern accommodations
and amusements (especially formal entertainments
that required the purchase of tickets).

Clark, Travels, II, #131

228. Watson, David (1773-1830)

MS Diary, 1796-1805. Alderman Library. Film
Colonial Williamsburg.

Major Watson was a state legislator from
Louisa County and a member of the first Board of
Visitors of the University of Virginia. He was
educated at the College of William and Mary,
1796-1797.

Only fragments of his diary have been pre-
served. This lume contains two pages describing his arrival at the college and his early impressions of life in Williamsburg--professors,
courses, textbooks and other required reading,
expenses and amusements.

229. Watson, Elkanah (1758-1842)

Men and Times of the Revolution; or, Memoirs of
Elkanah Watson, including Journals of Travels in
Europe and America, from 1777 to 1842....Ed. by
Winslow C. Watson. New York: Dana and Co., 1856.
460 p.

Young Watson spent the early years of the
Revolution in Providence, Rhode Island, where
he was apprenticed to the merchant John Brown.
He made his Southern tour in 1777 when the Browns
entrusted him with a responsible and dangerous
errand in Charleston, South Carolina, delivering
$50,000 to their agents there. With a good horse
under him, a hanger at his side, a pair of pistols
in his holster, and the money securely quilted into
the lining of his coat, he made the trip safely in
seventy-five days. After delivering the funds, he
journeyed through South Carolina and Georgia on a
sight-seeing tour. When he returned to Providence
after an absence of eight months, he had traveled
2700 miles.

In Virginia he traveled through Leesburg,
Fredericksburg, Williamsburg, Jamestown and Suffolk,
and returned by the same route. His Memoirs, written
years later and edited after his death by Winslow
Watson, his son, were based on a journal (which has
disappeared) with his reminiscences "improved" by
his son. His descriptions of places visited are
therefore less precise than the historian would
like them and more a matter of his general impressions than exact detail.

Clark, Travels, I, #324

230. Webster, Noah (1758-1843)

"Diary, 1785-1786," in Mrs. Emily Ellsworth Ford,
comp., Notes on the Life of Noah Webster....(New
York: Privately printed, 1912), I, 122-171.

Webster came South on a lecture tour, arriving in Richmond in November of 1785. He spent the first week of December in Williamsburg, then returned to Maryland via Richmond and Alexandria. He admired many individual Virginians (notably Washington, whom he visited several times at Mount Vernon) but was disappointed with their luke-warm reception of his lectures and attributed their "inattention" to fondness for dissipation, contempt for Yankess, little money and great pride. In Williamsburg he commented favorably on the beauty of the city, the college, the church and the Capitol--all rapidly decaying--and on George Wythe, "a great man for Virginia, and a sensible man anywhere."

Clark, Travels, II, #91

231. Weld, Isaac (1774-1856)

Travels through the States of North America, and the Provinces of Upper and Lower Canada, during the Years 1795, 1796, and 1797. 4th ed. London: John Stockdale, 1807. 2 vols.

Young Weld, son of a well-to-do minister in Dublin, came to America at the age of twenty-one to complete his education, and when he returned to Ireland he wrote a book about his travels. He later enjoyed a good reputation as a topographer and served for many years as an officer in the Royal Dublin Society.

He traveled through Pennsylvania, New York, New Jersey, Delaware, Maryland and Virginia and then went to Canada. He was enthusiastic about the scenery (the forests, Niagara Falls and Natural Bridge in particular) but critical of American manners. In Virginia he visited and described Alexandria, Mount Vernon, the Northern Neck, Gloucester, Yorktown, Williamsburg, Hampton, Norfolk, the Dismal Swamp, Richmond, Petersburg, Monticello and the Shenandoah Valley.

For the area above Richmond his descriptions borrow heavily from Jefferson's Notes; and though he visited and admired Mount Vernon, he used other sources for his description of it. In his comments on Virginia people he emphasized backwoodsmen and the lower classes in Tidewater: their sallow complexions, their love of hard liquor, barbecues and gambling at billiards, faro, cock fights and horse races. He was annoyed by the unattractive appearance of Virginia women (further disfigured by sunbonnets) and of men on horseback--the saddle was too close to the horse's mane and the horse traveled at a wrack or pace instead of the more "natural" trot. Nothing in Williamsburg pleased him. The disintegrating public buildings presented "a melancholy picture." College students were little boys who dined at President Madison's table without coats, shoes or stockings and "during dinner they constantly rose to help themselves at the sideboard. A couple of dishes of salted meat, and some oyster soup, formed the whole of the dinner." He mentioned these details, he declared, to "convey some little idea of American colleges and American dignitaries."

Clark, Travels, II, #132

232. Wellford, Robert (1753-1823)

"A Diary Kept by Dr. Robert Wellford, of Fredericksburg, Virginia, during the March of the Virginia Troops to Fort Pitt to Suppress the Whiskey Insurrection in 1794," William and Mary Quarterly, 1st ser., XI (1902), 1-19

After brief service with the British army in America as surgeon of the First Battalion of Grenadiers, Dr. Wellford resigned to practice medicine in Philadelphia. After the war was over he came to Fredericksburg with his friend Col. John Spotswood and lived there until his death. No diary has survived except the single unit describing the trip to Pittsburgh in 1794.

233. Whitefield, George (1714-1770)

The Works of the Reverend George Whitefield....
London: Printed for E. and C. Dilly, 1771-72.
7 vols.

Between the years 1738 and 1770 Whitefield
made seven missionary journeys to America and
preached all along the coast from Savannah to
Boston. During each visit he stopped at least
once at Savannah, where his orphans' home was
located, but he came to Williamsburg only once.
He arrived in town on Friday, December 14, 1739.
The next day he dined with Governor Gooch, who
received him "most courteously," and listened to
an edifying sermon by Commissary Blair, who acted
as his guide on a tour of the college and invited
him to preach the following day. He was favorably
impressed with the College of William and Mary,
where he found two Oxford contemporaries on the
faculty, but disappointed with the size of the
congregation when he preached on Sunday morning.

The reader is equally disappointed with
Whitefield's journal. Despite the fact that he
was one of the most effective evangelists of all
time, his writing does not have any of the spell-
binding qualities of his preaching.

Clark, Travels, I, #177

234. Wild, Ebenezer (1758-1794)

The Journal of Ebenezer Wild (1776-1781)....
Cambridge, Massachusetts: Massachusetts Historical
Society, 1891. 85 p. Also in Massachusetts Historical Society Proceedings, 2nd ser., VI (1890-91),
78-160.

Wild served throughout the war with the Massachusetts Line, and his journal covers the whole
period. His matter-of-fact account of the Virginia
campaign is interesting and valuable for the routine
of camp life and daily marches.

Clark, Travels, I, #326

235. Williamson, Peter (1730-1799)

Some Considerations on the Present State of
Affairs...[With] a Short Description...of the
Several Colonies on the Continent of North-
America....York, England: Printed for the Author,
1758.   56 p.

   Although the author was writing from his own
observation, because he had "travelled thro' all
these Countries," his descriptions are too brief
to be of much use.

Clark, Travels, I, #327

236. Wilson, Thomas (1655?-1725)

A Brief Journal of the Life, Travels, and Labours
of Love in the Work of the Ministry, of that Emi-
nent and Faithful Servant of Jesus Christ, Thomas
Wilson....Dublin: S. Fuller, 1728.   98 p.   Also in
Friends' Library, II (1838), 310-360.

   This Irish Quaker made two missionary journeys
to America--one in 1691, the other in 1714.   Both
times he visited Quakers in Virginia, where he had
"comfortable meetings" in spite of the difficulties
of travel and the contrary influence of George Keith's
friends.   On the second journey Wilson left Dublin
with another Quaker, James Dickinson, who had friends
in Virginia.   Their ship entered Lynhaven Bay and
landed them on the southern shore of the Rappahannock,
whence they crossed the peninsula on horseback, took
a borrowed boat across the York River, and started
south on foot, carrying their saddles and saddlebags.
They met a friend of Dickinson (also a Friend) on the
road; he dismounted and let them have his horse for
the journey into North Carolina.

Clark, Travels, I, #180

237. Woolman, John (1720-1772)

The Journal of John Woolman. Ed. by Janet Whitney.
Chicago: Henry Regnery Co., 1950. 233 p.

Woolman was greatly loved and admired by his
contemporaries for his simplicity and gentle charm.
His missionary travels brought him into the
Shenandoah Valley in the spring of 1746, and he
returned to Virginia in 1757 for the Yearly Meeting
in Isle of Wight County.

Instead of a record of the details of his
journeys, his journal is a series of essays, reflections on recent trips seemingly recorded after
he had returned to New Jersey. In the Virginia
essays he was entirely concerned with slavery--the
moral and physical conditions of the slaves and the
vicious effects of the system on the planters, who
had received him hospitably enough but lived "in
ease on the toil of their slaves."

Clark, Travels, I, #181

INDEX TO WILLIAMSBURG DATA

Sixty of these travelers in the Tidewater described visits to Williamsburg with enough comment on the town, the people, and their way of life to provide a valuable collection of historical sources. The following subject index to Williamsburg data in their records has been prepared in the hope that it may prove useful to other members of the Research Department.

WILLIAMSBURG

WILLIAMSBURG

WILLIAMSBURG

Inns (cont'd)
        signs, 195
        Southall's, 227
        Stith's, Mrs., 43, 125
        Sullivan's, Mrs., 43
        Trebell's, 227
        Vobe's, Mrs., 6, 227
        Wetherburn's, 227

James City Courhouse, 13, 70, 119, 125, 134, 157, 195
        portico columns "lost", 134
Jefferson, Gov. Thomas
        treatment of Henry Hamilton, 107
Jenings, Edmund, 43, 150

Lafayette's headquarters in, 23
Lectures in, 230
Lee, Philip Ludwell, 83
Lightning rods, use of, 62
Living expenses in, 61, 70, 195
Location, 112, 181, 215, 230
        advantages of, 125, 150
        disadvantages of, 33, 102, 128, 157, 183, 195
        in two counties, 125
Lotteries, 229

McClurg, Dr. James, 195

Madison, Bishop James, 119, 228
        library, 133
Market place, 102, 125, 133
Merchant activity in, 195
Meteorological tables for 1772-77, 124
Methodists in, 149
"Metropolis, The," 76, 83, 102, 206
Military garrison in, 70
Missionaries in, 126, 167, 196, 212
Monroe, Col. [James?], 139
Murray, John, Earl of Dunmore, 76

WILLIAMSBURG

WILLIAMSBURG